A Taste of

UPSTATE
NEW YORK

Generously supported by

A gift in honor of

Elizabeth Pfeiffer

A Taste of
UPSTATE
NEW YORK

THE PEOPLE AND THE STORIES
BEHIND 40 FOOD FAVORITES

CHUCK D'IMPERIO

SYRACUSE UNIVERSITY PRESS

∞ The paper used in this publication meets the minimum requirements
of the American National Standard for Information Sciences—Permanence
of Paper for Printed Library Materials, ANSI Z39.48-1992.

Unless otherwise specified all photographs appearing in this volume are courtesy of the author.

For a listing of books published and distributed by Syracuse University Press,
visit www.SyracuseUniversityPress.syr.edu.

ISBN: 978-0-8156-1049-6 (paper)   978-0-8156-5323-3 (e-book)

Library of Congress Cataloging-in-Publication Data
D'Imperio, Chuck.
A taste of Upstate New York : the people and the stories behind forty food favorites /
Chuck D'Imperio. — First edition.
pages cm
Includes index.
ISBN 978-0-8156-1049-6 (pbk. : alk. paper) — ISBN 978-0-8156-5323-3 (e-book)
1. Food—New York (State) —New York—Guidebooks.   2. Food—New York
(State) —New York—Anecdotes.   3. New York (N.Y.) —Guidebooks.   I. Title.
TX907.3.N72D56 2015
641.59747—dc23   2014048605

Manufactured in the United States of America

To the future:
My grandson, Connor Ray Duncan

CHUCK D'IMPERIO is the author of several books about Upstate New York. His most recent titles from Syracuse University Press include *The Unknown Museums of Upstate New York: A Guide to 50 Treasures* (2013), and *Monumental New York: A Guide to 30 Iconic Memorials in Upstate New York* (2011). He is a longtime radio broadcaster with Townsquare Media Radio in Oneonta (since 1989) and has contributed hundreds of travel articles, newspaper columns, and magazine articles to media both locally and nationally. In 2000 he was inducted into the New York State Country Music Hall of Fame as New York's "Broadcaster of the Year." In 2011 he was the recipient of the prestigious New York State DAR Motion Picture, Radio and Television Award for being an "Eminent Upstate New York Historian, Award-Winning Broadcaster and Celebrated Book Author and Newspaper Columnist." Chuck is married to Trish, an educator, and they are the proud parents of Frances, Katie, Abby and Joey. They live, of course, in Upstate New York.

CONTENTS

One for the History Books

Upstate Food Traditions

The Upstate New York Food Hall of Fame

Delicious Upstate New York Destinations

INTRODUCTION

*T*his book is the third in my Upstate New York series for Syracuse University Press. My first book was a guide to some of the iconic memorials and statues which dot the area's landscape. The most recent book explored fifty smaller "unknown" museums of the region. Both were fun and fascinating books to research and write.

This book, however, was *delicious*!

I have lived in various parts of the country over the years and have always enjoyed the "food trail" to parts unknown. While living in Washington, DC, for several years, I got to know and love the unique tastes found in the small towns and back roads of Northern Virginia. My many years living in Los Angeles introduced me to Southwestern and Asian foods. Five years in Houston gave me a hankering for Tex-Mex and all kinds of barbecue. Several years in New York City initiated my love for the side street deli and the ubiquitous food cart vendors always underfoot. I have loved it all.

But I am a true son of Upstate New York, and I finally came to appreciate the variety of special foods and tastes that can be found all over my home region. From the Hudson Valley to the St. Lawrence Seaway, and from James Fenimore Cooper's Leatherstocking region to the Finger Lakes and beyond, Upstate New York is truly a multifaceted jewel for those of us who enjoy eating and exploring different foods.

While the gastronomical wonders of New York City have been the subject of hundreds of books and thousands of articles, Upstate New York is not without its own wonders and quirky food facts. I mean, did you know that Binghamton is the Home of Oleomargarine? Of course not. Nobody knows that. But in fact Henry W. Bradley patented the gooey alternative to butter in Binghamton in 1871. Or did you know that superchef Rachel Ray got her start fixing "Meals in a Minute" at an upscale market in an Albany strip mall? Or that the club sandwich was invented at the Canfield Casino in Saratoga Springs in 1894?

Have you ever been to Phelps, population two thousand? Once proclaimed the Sauerkraut Capital of the World, this community still holds an annual Sauerkraut Festival featuring the crowning of a Kraut King and Queen and the divvying up of the ceremonial sauerkraut cake.

Make a visit to the exquisite Onteora Mountain House Bed and Breakfast in Boiceville. This magnificent mansion sits on a promontory overlooking the Catskill Mountains and has been called one of the most beautiful inns in the United States. Seeing this out-of-the-way gem makes you appreciate what money can buy. Mayonnaise money, that is. Yes, this mansion was once the home of Richard Hellman, the mayonnaise millionaire. At the other end of the compass, in Gouverneur, city fathers found Edward Noble's impact on their community so significant that they raised a towering monument to him in the village green. The monument? An eight-foot-long replica of a pack of Pep-O-Mint Lifesavers. Noble, the candy's creator, was born here.

And while there are a lot of food firsts in our area, there is also at least one famous "food last." Tucked away in the High Peaks of the Adirondacks you will find the very last orange-roofed Howard Johnson's restaurant in the country. Of more than a thousand restaurants in the early 1970s, this final one is still open at 2099 Saranac Road in Lake Placid. It has been quite a ride for this popular, family-friendly place, which sold twenty-eight flavors of ice cream and gave the American eating public their first taste of fried clam strips. I was so struck by the sheer nostalgia of this slice of Americana that I gave it its own chapter.

In this book you will find the story of forty food favorites from the Upstate region. Actually, you will find the story of forty *people* who bring their food favorites to us all. You will meet the Catskill Mountains Candy Cane King, the Father of the Chicken Nugget, and the Queen of the Grape Pie, as well as the black dirt farmers of Orange County who give America its best-tasting onions.

We'll travel to the birthplace of pie à la mode as well as the city that gave us our favorite Super Bowl snack, chicken wings. We'll stop in Saratoga, where potato chips originated, and we'll make a side trip to the Southern Tier, where spiedies were born.

We'll meet colorful characters like Charlie the Butcher, purveyor of the best beef on weck in Upstate, and Cider Mill Bill, who cheerily oversees one of the state's most popular working cider mills in a place called Fly Creek. I'll introduce you to Pete Donnelly, who has been serving up ice cream from the same stand in Saranac Lake for more than sixty years, all the while using the same, original equipment. We'll make a quick stop in Mexico, New York, for some of Grandma Brown's Home Baked Beans, and then shoot up to the birthplace of Thousand Island dressing. You'll meet Blaine Campany, the owner of a legendary bologna shop in the Tug Hill Plateau. We will even make a brief visit to New York's northernmost ski resort for a plate of the best poutine you will ever have.

You *have* heard of poutine, haven't you?

These are the stories of our childhood. Moist black-and-white half moon cookies with a glass of milk on a hot summer day. Steaming salt potatoes at a backyard picnic. A plate full of mini hot dogs slathered in Greek sauce. Ice cream sundaes on the way home from church. A juicy hamburger shared with friends at a country drive-in. All of them have their very roots in Upstate New York.

I chased down a lot of stories about food favorites for this book. Most of those stories you will find within the pages of *A Taste of Upstate New York*. Others were a little trickier. Let me explain.

One fun story I tried to unearth was the origin of an unusual appetizer in the Capital District: mozzarella sticks with raspberry sauce. Sounds like a weird combination, doesn't it? I'd heard about it since I went to college in Albany the 1960s. I was able to find it in a few Albany-area restaurants, and I have had it several times at Ralph's Tavern on Central Avenue. It was good. Odd, but good. So I wondered, who came up with the idea of mixing these two items together? Where did it start? Was it a mistake that just seemed to catch on? Why will you not find it outside of the Albany-Schenectady-Troy area? Unfortunately, this dish is like a ghost, or a food

Yes, it is a weird combination! Mozzarella sticks and raspberry sauce can only be found in the Capital District.

fog. The answers may be out there somewhere, but I was unable to find anybody who knows where mozzarella sticks with raspberry sauce came from, so the story remains untold in this book.

Another Upstate favorite I kept running across was the famed Peppermint Pigs of Saratoga. These delightful Victorian Christmas treats have graced the tables of Upstaters for decades. However, is a sugary peppermint candy pig served one day a year really a food? I don't know. The tradition is wonderful though. Saratoga Sweets makes them by the thousands. Shiny little Peppermint Pigs served in tiny sacks, accompanied by a miniature hammer. The host passes the candy sow around the table and people take a whack at the pig until there is nothing left in the sack but sugary smithereens. Then everybody eats the pieces and toasts to good fortunes in the new year. It is sweet and charming and definitely an Upstate tradition, but I really didn't know where to mention it in this book.

I just did.

Lyons was once the center of all peppermint production in the East.

And speaking of peppermint, I almost devoted an entire chapter to a village. That's right, an entire village. Lyons, known as the Peppermint Village, is located in the western part of the state (Wayne County), and it was once the home of Hotchkiss Essential Oil Company, one of the nation's leading makers of peppermint extract. It is said that back in the 1800s, when the company was really cranking it out, the whole town smelled like it had been kissed by peppermint. They have had peppermint festivals in the past to pay tribute to what was once the village's leading export.

Some might argue that New York State maple syrup deserves its own chapter in this book. For sure, few states can match the creamy springtime sweetness of Upstate syrup, and it really is one of the fastest growing agribusinesses in the region. Many farms now have their own little retail shops selling maple products, and maple festivals abound when the sap is running. Look for the Empire State to one day be the leader in maple production. But for now we are still chasing Vermont, which produces three times as many gallons of syrup as New York.

Submarine sandwiches almost got a nod in the book, too. These meals on a roll are pretty much a staple of Upstate. Sure, they can be found across the country now, but many of the earliest sub chains began in our region. These latter day Dagwoods come by all different names in different regions of the state: submarines, hoagies, heroes, and grinders. Many swear that Jreck Subs reigns supreme as the best submarine chain in Upstate. You will get no argument from me on that.

Chobani yogurt has become the number one Greek yogurt in America with blinding speed. The manufacturing plant for Chobani is located in a pristine, bucolic corner of rural Chenango County. Was New York State ever known for its yogurt? No. But since 2005 it has been, and each package of Chobani carries with it the proud name of New Berlin, New York, on the side. In this little town of no more than 2,500 people, Chobani employs 1,250 workers. Who would have dreamed that the headquarters of the country's leading Greek yogurt maker would be here, in the middle of nowhere? Nobody.

Did you know that Upstate New York has produced perhaps the best-tasting onions in America for more than a century? And that they come from an area carrying the odd moniker Black Dirt Region? Take a ride through Orange County sometime during growing season and check out the miles of luscious juicy onions ready to pop. And be sure to bring a hankie along to wipe your tear-stained cheeks! The rich, black dirt found around the hamlet of Pine Island is the result of glaciers scraping up the bottomland as they retreated millennia ago. The area, relatively small (26,000 acres), is considered to have some of the richest farmland in the country. It was producing more than thirty thousand pounds of onions *per acre* during the late 1800s. Today the area has diversified its harvest, utilizing the rich black soil to produce award-winning tomatoes, carrots, and lettuce. Andrew Gurda's farm and stand is one of the most popular showcases for these truly remarkable vegetables.

Early German, Dutch, and Polish immigrants realized the potential of this area's unique sulfur- and nitrogen-rich soil, and it was they who planted the first onions here around 1910. During the harvest, teams of onion pickers descend on the area picking and packing the sweet yellow orbs. How is this for some Upstate trivia? It has been reported that when the land is raked here to prepare for planting that you can see the "black scar" that the plowing produces from the NASA satellites floating thousands of miles above the earth!

And while we are at it, whose idea was it to first roll up a pizza? Many will tell you that pizza rolls were first invented to satiate the cravings of overserved college students in the 1970s in Canton, New York. Local favorite Sergi's Canton Italian is still the destination for late night revelers seeking out the unique pleasures of a "fat bag" to top the night off.

As the author of this book, I had a free rein in picking and choosing each entry. Some of these entries are must-haves in any book on food favorites of Upstate, including such venerable dishes as hamburgers, chicken riggies, pusties, and chicken wings. Others are included in the book because their stories are so wonderful, so charming, that I just couldn't help but share them with you. Like the story of Richard Ecklof, who gave away more than a million of his specialty cookies over the years. Yes, you heard me. *Gave away.*

Another positively charming story I could not resist, and one that is clearly outside the bounds of being a food, is the story of the Crystal Bar and Restaurant in Watertown. I think you will agree that its chapter, concerning a legendary holiday tradition, is one of the most delightful in the book.

As I wrote this book, my quest was to travel as far as I could, sample as much as I could, and track down as many delicious morsels of Upstate food information as possible. In addition to presenting specific foods from different regions of the state, I have created several thematic sections of the book for your enjoyment. One section is focused on traditions that hold a special place in Upstate New York culture. Another section highlights the most iconic food favorites scattered across the state—the hamburger, chicken wings, Jell-O, ice cream sundaes, and potato chips. And the Delicious Upstate New York Destinations section is devoted to some remarkable one-of-a-kind restaurants and many of the varied food festivals held in Upstate. As I do with all of my Upstate books, I must preempt any persnickety reader who might take exception to the broad sweep of my use of the term *Upstate*. I use this term generically to reflect the fact that my books, my work, my research, and my passion are all based on the areas of New York State that do not include the five boroughs of New York City. There are far more gifted chroniclers than I who can take up this topic for those regions' readers. Trust me, I really do know where Upstate is. I was born here.

My journey, as you can see, has taken me thousands of miles across a wide area. I was in the Hudson Valley in the spring, in the Finger Lakes during fall festival season, in the Adirondacks through the snowfall, and in the bigger cities of Albany, Buffalo, Rochester, Syracuse, Binghamton, Kingston, and Utica in the summer. I think I have really seen it all, through many shades of glasses, and it has been a great ride.

One frustrating aspect of writing such a book is my tendency to want to feature my own hometown, to showcase the foods that I love and enjoy frequently. I live in Oneonta (Otsego County), which is near the geographical center of the state. It is hard not to highlight my own favorite food hangouts. And although I have not included any of my hometown's restaurants in the chapters of this book, there are a couple that I simply must mention.

Oneonta has a rich food history. We have two fine restaurants that are housed in old, restored railroad train stations: The Depot and Stella Luna's. Both have stayed true to the historic railroad legacy of Oneonta, which was at one time home to the world's largest railroad roundhouse. And it was in this town, in 1883, that a group of eight men met in a little red caboose and formed the first national railroad workers union in the United States. That little caboose is now enshrined in our city park.

Brooks' House of BBQ is located in Oneonta. Run by the Brooks family for more than seventy years, it is perhaps the most historic family barbecue place in the state. Here, Griff and Frances Brooks began selling their barbecue chicken in 1958 under the giant screen of the Del-Sego Drive-In. Today the restaurant features the longest indoor charcoal barbecue pit in the East (38 feet). Thousands eat there every year, from locals who meet routinely for lunch to the big tourist buses that pull in and release fifty at a time to the savory aroma of Brooks' famous barbecued chickens.

Oneonta is the home of two major colleges, and over the many years, tens of thousands of students have come and gone through its city limits.

All of them have eaten at and enjoyed themselves at Brooks', and after graduation they have scattered to the four corners of the country (and the world) carrying with them great memories of what many consider to be Upstate's top barbecue restaurant. In fact, when Hillary Clinton announced her intention to run for the U.S. Senate seat from New York, she capped off the event with a photo op of her chowing down on a big piece of Brooks' chicken.

My hometown is also the location of many pizza parlors, which is nothing unusual in New York. There seems to be one on every corner. Having sampled all of them, many times, I can tell you that Oneonta makes a slice as good as you will find anywhere. But there is one pizza joint that I must tell you about.

Tino's is located right in the heart of Main Street. This pizza parlor has been a part of the Oneonta scene for more than thirty five years. Their specialty is cold cheese pizza. In fact, many references both in the media and online refer to Tino's as the Original Home of the Cold Cheese Pizza. Sure you can get it at most parlors now, but many believe it all started right here.

Their cold cheese pizza is a wonder to behold. I know. I've "beheld" it many times.

A generous slice of pizza crust is painted thickly with a tangy red sauce. And then the cold cheese. Big, thick shavings of cold mozzarella literally piled on top of your hot slice. It really takes a simple slice of pizza and turns it into a meal and a half. Tino's cold cheese pizza is a favorite of all Oneontans and many others who simply come here trying to find out what the heck a "cold cheese slice" really is. They'll find it, the original, at Tino's in my hometown.

It is my hope that this book acts as a virtual food map of the Upstate New York region. There have been many attempts to map out the most popular food favorites over the years. In fact, there are many culinary maps on the Internet even today.

One example that I stumbled upon really tells an amazing story not only of New York's changing tastes, but those of America as well. The map, published in the November 26, 1933, edition of California's *Oakland Tribune* newspaper, illustrated in great detail the food favorites of each state. The remarkable thing about this map is that it was drawn up when our country was in the throes of the Great Depression. And that was clearly evident by some of the prominent poor man's food favorites depicted inside each state.

In Nevada, for example, the food favorite at the time was carrot pudding. In Wyoming it was something called potato moulds. Mississippians favored flannel cakes, and Pennsylvanians enjoyed pepper pots. The top 1933 food sensation in West Virginia was a delightful dish called pigeons in cornmeal.

Curiously, the only two Upstate New York foods illustrated in this 1933 tableau are lobster Newburgh (in Western New York) and "noodles and ham" in the North Country.

Noodles and ham?

I found it strange that the author of this article identified our Upstate region with a food that is distinctly not a Depression-era dish (lobster Newburgh), and the other a food nobody has really ever heard of (noodles and ham).

I have met many culinary legends during my three-thousand-mile trip around Upstate in researching this book. It has been fun. Everybody is a cook. Some make it big and have nationally recognized food dishes named after them. Others specialize in a distinct dish of their own that is popular in a small, focused area. Others just make their item and sell it because they love it. From Grandma's spaghetti sauce to Uncle Harry's boloney to your own homemade desserts, there is no shortage of food favorites in our area.

One of the most pleasant memories from my year-long food journey for this book happened completely by surprise. And yes, it is proof that everybody is a cook in Upstate New York.

I was traveling through downtown Utica one day, always on the lookout for a food story, when I came across a roadblock in the street. Highway construction was about to send me off into the unknown. Before I could fire up my trusty GPS, I was traveling through neighborhoods and areas of Utica I'd never seen before. I turned a corner and started down a street that was a mixture of boarded up storefronts and mixed-use housing.

And then I saw it.

A barber shop. And in the front window was a sign that read "Bean Pies Sold Here." Bean pies? How unusual! How unique! How gross! How could I not stop?

I parked and walked in to what was clearly an African American barber shop. I felt like I was walking in on the taping of an old Bill Cosby show. There were old timers sitting around in well-worn leatherette chairs chatting away. They were laughing and smiling their gold-toothed smiles, slapping backs and guffawing at each other's oft-heard jokes. A couple of young men were hunched over a chess board, hat bills pointed behind them. A jazzy mixture of Dizzy Gillespie and 1960s calypso music was emanating from an old boom box on the counter. And the owner, a large man with Don King hair, was sitting in the middle barber chair holding court. I announced my presence and the reason for stopping by and was met with silence. The old guys in the chairs said a hasty farewell to the owner, and the younger men brought an end to their chess game.

I introduced myself to the owner, Muhammad X Seven. He was an older gent who favored a leg. I asked him about his bean pies.

"Never heard of them before, have you?" he asked me with a cautious smile on his face. He then began to wax eloquent about his homemade navy bean pies, which he'd been making for years. "I sell them right out of this barber shop," he said. "Sometimes people even stop me on the street out front and ask if I have any. It is a Muslim dish, mostly. But all people really like them around the holidays."

I assured Mr. Seven that I had never heard of a bean pie before. "You don't know what you are missing," he laughed.

Unfortunately, he was out of pies when I stopped by. "I gotta bake me up some this weekend," he confided. He was a friendly old guy who warmed to me quickly. I shared laughs and stories from the road with him, and he told me many of his own favorite food stories. As I left, he handed me one of his homemade business cards. "King-Queen Pies," it read.

"It's because of all the chess that gets played in here," he said with a wink.

I asked him for a photograph. He agreed. I watched him lumber out of his barber chair, limp to the back of the shop, and begin to brush down his good-sized head of hair. "I want to look good for you, sir," he said.

After the hair brushing he opened up a small locker and took out a coat. It was a pristine white chef's coat. "King-Queen Pies" read the stitching over the front pocket. He took off his barber's apron and donned the chef coat. He pressed down the creases with his big hands and said, "There, that's nice."

I thought how lucky I was to stumble upon this little out-of-the-way place. While Dinosaur Bar-B-Que may sell tons of baby back ribs, and Lupo's may grill thousands of pounds of spiedies, this guy probably sells a couple of dozen homemade navy bean pies each year. But they are *his* pies, and he couldn't be prouder.

I helped him down the rickety front steps of the building and asked him to stand in front of the window sign that read: "Muhammad's Barber Shop. Bean Pies Sold Here. Eye Brows Waxed." I could see all the older gents who had evacuated the shop when I entered now standing off to one side giggling and poking good-natured fun at the barber. As Muhammad raised up on his good leg, gave a final pat down to his hair, and then stood perfectly still, I chuckled to myself, "The Bean Pie King. How great is this?"

A couple of things you should know about this book before you head out on a sampling tour of Upstate. I fully realize that I have merely scratched the surface, in an infinitesimal way, regarding the food favorites of Upstate New York. This book is really just one man's opinion, my own singular journal of good tastes, good times, and good people. With this in mind, let's use this book as a starting point, a jumping off point for a food discussion. An appetizer, if you will.

In anticipation of a large number of readers wanting to share their own food favorites with me, I cordially invite you to visit and contribute to my Facebook page at www.facebook.com/atasteofupstatenewyork. On this page, we can all share our stories of food traditions, food favorites, unknown restaurants, and happy eating memories from our region. And I fully expect a robust discussion about the first inductees into what I call my "Upstate New York Food Hall of Fame" (chapters 36–40).

One of my greatest food discoveries, the Bean Pie King in Utica.

Who would you have nominated?

So, here we go. Loosen your belts and grab the Rolaids. It is upward and onward to the land we love, the land of the Garbage Plate, the home of apple sausage, the birthplace of Meatballs in a Heel, and beyond.

A land we call Upstate New York.

Mangia!

ABOUT THE REGIONS

*T*his book is divided into eight regions (and their counties) for simplicity of reference:

> *Chautauqua/Allegany*: Chautauqua, Allegany, Cattaraugus
> *Greater Niagara*: Erie, Niagara, Orleans, Genesee, Wyoming.
> *Finger Lakes*: Monroe, Livingston, Steuben, Cayuga, Wayne, Ontario, Yates, Schuyler, Seneca, Tioga, Onondaga, Cortland, Tompkins
> *Thousand Islands/Seaway*: Oswego, Jefferson, St. Lawrence
> *Central Leatherstocking*: Otsego, Broome, Chenango, Madison, Montgomery, Oneida, Schoharie
> *Adirondacks/North Country*: Franklin, Clinton, Essex, Herkimer, Hamilton, Warren, Fulton, Lewis
> *Catskills/Hudson Valley*: Delaware, Greene, Ulster, Sullivan, Columbia, Dutchess, Putnam, Westchester, Orange, Rockland
> *Capital District/Saratoga*: Albany, Rensselaer, Schenectady, Saratoga, Washington

The regions are arranged in sequence so that the places described in each chapter are in close geographic proximity to those described in the preceding or following chapter. This positioning will allow readers to create their own itinerary for a food visit to, say, Buffalo or the Albany area.

All information in this book has been verified to be accurate as of the date of publication. Readers are advised when exploring this subject matter, as in all travels, to call ahead or check online to make sure their destination is open.

New York State Regions

1,000 Islands/ Seaway

Greater Niagara

Finger Lakes

Chautauqua/ Allegany

0   50

Miles

Syracuse University Cartographic Laboratory

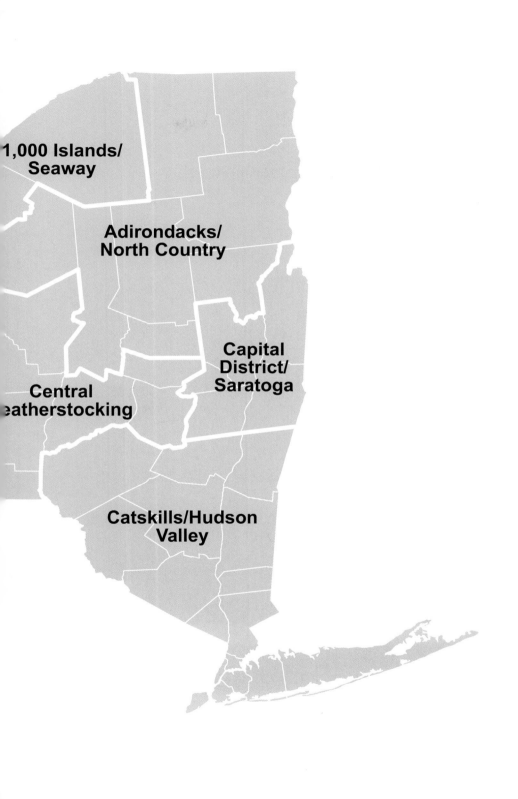

Region One

CHAUTAUQUA/ALLEGANY

Chautauqua, Allegany, Cattaraugus

1

PINK STRIPED COOKIES

Jamestown

*I*n the mid- to late 1800s, one out of every five Swedes left their homeland to come to America. Sweden was emptied of more than a million natives in a span of about fifty years. Most of these new immigrants settled in the Chicago and Minnesota areas. Many others planted themselves in Western New York. It was here in Jamestown, beyond the rolling Finger Lakes and just northwest of Pennsylvania's coal country, that the industrious Swedes left an indelible mark with their foods, religions, culture, and traditions.

More often than not Swedish was the language used in the small one-room school houses of the region. The pickled fish meals, the colorful floral bonnets, the lilting sounds of the nyckelharpa, and the smells of the baking fruit breads of the old country were all a part of rural Western New York life.

"The breads are heavily flavored with spices you just don't find in baked goods much anymore," Richard Ecklof told me. He is the owner of Ecklof Bakery in Jamestown, one of the oldest "from scratch" bakeries in New York State. "At our bakery we use a lot of almond flavoring, almond paste, and cardamom in our breads. A lot of the old Swedish families come in regularly for it. It reminds them of the good old days. Of home. At one time there were a dozen or more little Swedish bakeries in Jamestown. Now it is just us. We are the last free-standing Swedish bakery in the area."

Richard began working in this bakery when he was ten years old. It was his father's place, and he grew up surrounded by the wonderful aroma of the Swedish baked goods that were made from his grandfather's recipes. "My grandfather, David, came right over from Sweden to Jamestown

3

The pink striped cookie from Ecklof's Bakery is a Western New York tradition.

where he opened up a traditional bakery. I was mopping floors in here when I was a little kid. Now I have a family of my own and my son Chad runs the place with me. In fact when I retire he will take over as yet another in a long line of Ecklof bakers in the area," the sixty-four-year-old said.

Ecklof Bakery has changed quite a bit since Grandpa kneaded his first batch of Swedish Limpa. They now serve lunches, have a deli, and have a full service kitchen. Of course the bakery is still what they are known for. "My dad started his own bakery when he got out of the service after World War II. We stayed at one location for almost fifty years. A decade ago we had to move a block away and open up another, bigger place. We went from three thousand square feet to almost five thousand square feet. It's a busy place," Richard said.

If there is anything this legendary bakery has made over the decades that still rings true with the thousands who have come through the front door of Ecklof's, it is the pink striped cookie.

"When my Dad opened up in 1956, he made these little cakey pink striped cookies. He had them on the counter for sale, but he was always giving them away to the little kids who came in with their mothers. Soon the cookies were a well embedded tradition that is still carried on in the shop," he said. "There is no magical secret to the cookie. My father bought a cookie machine at a food show in the 1950s and the cookie recipe came with the machine. It's kind of like a cross between shortbread and a sugar cookie. We put a pink stripe of icing down the middle and people just love them. We make one hundred dozen a day and they are by far the most popular item we have at Ecklof's."

I asked him about carrying on the tradition of handing out a free pink striped cookie to the little ones. "Oh, yes. We have to. Only today it is more than likely to be a mother or even a grandmother who comes in with a child and they tell them about coming in fifty years ago getting their own free pink striped cookie. It is a nostalgic thing, mostly, and we couldn't be happier to make sure all the little ones get a cookie."

Ecklof's has made and sold *millions* of pink striped cookies over the years, and has given away countless more. "We sell them online and we believe that we have shipped the pink stripes to about thirty states as well as overseas. Many residents buy them to send to their sons and daughters who are serving throughout the world in the military. A lot of our mail order customers are folks from the Jamestown area who have moved away and love to receive a little memory from home once in a while. That little cookie does have its fans, for sure. In fact Jim Kelly, the former quarterback of the Buffalo Bills, really loves them a lot," he told me.

From Grandfather Ecklof to father to son and soon to grandson, the strain of love and familial ties lie deep within the walls of this old bakery in far Western New York.

"You know the old saying about something 'being in your blood?' Well, this bakery is definitely in my blood. It is so satisfying to me when I come in here early in the morning and start things up. To know that I am beginning with just a bunch of raw ingredients and that eventually throughout the day, we will be providing reliable, tasty and beloved items to our many customers is very gratifying. People share comments with us about how much they enjoy our product and our service. It makes me proud to know that we have given folks so many nice things they have enjoyed over the years. And that includes that little pink striped cookie!"

2

CUBA CHEESE
Cuba

*N*ew Yorkers love to "say cheese!"

The state ranks third in total cheese production in the United States, just behind Wisconsin (#1) and California. We make nearly a billion pounds of it annually. And while it is still a key component in the Empire State's agricultural output today, there is a lot of fascinating history to the cheese-making industry of the past.

New York State cheeses have won every award ever offered in the industry and have been a favorite of Americans since the early 1800s. Even President Andrew Jackson, a dyed-in-the-wool southerner, insisted on having New York State cheese stocked in the pantry of the White House all throughout his eight years in office. One time he ordered two thousand wheels of cheese at once just to make sure he never ran out.

Many of the state's cheese-making companies have been around since the infancy of the New York dairy industry. Herkimer Cheese has been churning out cheddar cheese for more than sixty years in the Mohawk Valley. German immigrant Leo Kutter opened up his first cheese factory in Corfu, east of Buffalo, nearly a century ago. Kutter's Cheese Factory is still there, excelling in producing the finest sharp, Muenster, Gouda, and Edam varieties.

William McCadam cut his first wheel of cheese on his kitchen table at his home in Heuvelton in 1876. From the kitchen to the ox cart to the Erie Canal, McCadam Cheese soon became one of the most widely known brand names of them all.

Thousands of tourists stop here every year to stock up on Cuba Cheese.

Jesse Williams founded America's first cheese factory in Rome in 1851. The largest wheel of cheese ever made was made in Upstate New York. It came from the Martinsburgh Cheese Factory in Central New York, and the cheese wheel was seven feet tall. It weighed two tons. The state has two cheese museums. As you can see, the history just keeps going and going.

Cuba Cheese is a wonderful cross section of history, pride, quality, and success. "The first cheese company was formed in Cuba in 1871, and in 1889, that plant was expanded to include three stories. That is the building we are still in," said Sarah Bradley, Vice President of Marketing and Advertising for the Cuba Cheese Shoppe. "There were dozens of dairy farms around this region and many people boasted that we made the best cheese in the state. Some attributed our famous cheddar cheeses to the characteristically rich flavor of the milk from our New York State cows. There is something in the soil and water out here in the Great Lakes area that makes our cheese sharp, buttery and unique."

The Cuba Cheese Shoppe no longer makes the cheese in their building, but they are the purveyors of some of the Northeast's best locally made dairy products. "We carry over 325 types of cheeses, mostly from Upstate New York but also from as far away as Italy and Germany. No matter how many items we sell, the New York State Extra Sharp Cheddar Cheese is far and away our best seller."

Sarah Bradley is the new face of the modern cheese industry. A young, attractive woman who is comfortably in charge of this vast retail operation, Sarah always has an eye on the future with a special recognition of the past. "Believe it or not, Cuba was once considered to be the 'Cheese Capital of the World.' We made lots of cheese around here and it was all of the finest quality. In the 1800s each week over at the Kinney Hotel on West Main Street (now gone) a group of old cheese barons would meet at the bar and settle upon the going price of cheese. They would then announce it to the world from the hotel's front porch and the price would be set until the following week. Hard to imagine that the going price for cheese around the world was set in a small hotel every week here in Cuba. Now that is history, and we take our role in the cheese industry here very seriously," she told me.

I asked her if there were any secrets in the Cuba Cheese Shoppe building.

"Oh, if these old walls could talk," she said with a smile. "For example, Old York cheddar cheese, horseradish and port wine spreads are extremely popular at our shop. They were first created and made right below our feet in the basement in the 1940s. The previous owners sold the recipe to Schriber Foods in Wisconsin. We know, and all of our regular customers know that even though the label says York is made in Wisconsin, the truth is it was invented right here in Cuba in our cellar."

Today the Cuba Cheese Shoppe is one of the largest such retail stores in New York. Sarah keeps a watchful eye on the myriad of local cheese products that come through here and get slapped with the Cuba Cheese Shoppe label.

"We have our regulars, for sure, but more and more people are finding us as we expand the store online and through the mail. My dad, Jeff Bradley, bought the business back in 1991. I am a graduate from the State University of New York in Brockport, and although I didn't start out active in the business, it just kind of happened that way. As a little kid I used to work out back with the ladies putting labels on the cheese. Before long I did it all. I even drove the cheese truck for a while. I sure put on a lot of miles," she laughed.

I asked Sarah if there is a cheese season.

"Yes, definitely Christmas. We have to hire extra people to work here. People to answer the phones, fill orders, package the cheese. We can crank out eight hundred packages a day just before Christmas. It is very exciting and very tiring. But we all work together and it can be fun."

The day I spent at the store I was struck by the various ages of the employees working the front counter, stocking the shelves, and slicing big blocks of cheese on the butcher block. "Yes, we have a varied and loyal group of people working for us," Bradley told me. "They are my friends. Every morning when I come in I grab a cup of coffee and go out and chat with 'my girls.' Some have been here a very long time. I know that they are the people our customers have to face each morning and they are all great."

With Dad still working the business (and brother Justin working as a truck driver, or as Sarah calls him, "my cheese peddler") this family business is not letting any grass grow under its collective feet. "I am very excited that we have a new place opened in nearby Ellicottville. It is a major ski resort town so I know the many national and international travelers who go there will find and enjoy the cheeses from Cuba and take our product out and spread the news even farther. It is very exciting."

Sarah Bradley is an engine of activity. A dynamo. I asked her if there was a secret to her drive and the shop's success. She reached across her desk and pulled off a little piece of yellow paper with some writing on it.

"This here is my Dad's work credo: 'Growth, Profitability Provide for the Future.' I believe in those words and work hard every day to live up to them. The Cuba Cheese Shoppe is a very special place. There is literally over a hundred years of history here. And that is important. People come in here and talk about coming in when they were younger. They all say that taking a bite out of some Cuba cheese is like a memory of home. I have lived and worked in some dreadful places in the past but when I come in here each morning, well, every day is a new day. I want to be here. I love it."

Oh, and the two cheese museums I mentioned? One is in Rome, New York, and the other one is . . . in Cuba!

Region Two

GREATER NIAGARA

Erie, Niagara, Orleans, Genesee, Wyoming

3

SPONGE CANDY

Buffalo

$\mathcal{F}$owler's Chocolates is as much a Buffalo tradition as hot wings, football, and record-setting snowfalls.

"This business has been around a lot longer than I have," owner Ted Marks told me. "It was incorporated in 1910 and was probably even around before that. The founder, Joe Fowler, was an Englishman who brought his recipes to America at the turn of the twentieth century. He set up his chocolate stand just outside the big Pan American Exposition in Buffalo and did quite well there, so I am told. Before long he opened up a candy store on the east side of Buffalo, and Fowler's stayed there until the 1960s when they moved to West Seneca."

So how did Ted Marks get interested in the business?

"Well, my only connection to candy was as a consumer," he laughed. "The Fowler family was running out of steam after several generations, and they were looking for new blood to get the company and their product up and ready for the future. So my father, Randy Marks, and I bought the company. I was the hands-on guy, and my dad, who passed away in 2012, was my biggest advisor and supporter."

Many of the candy items sold at Fowlers are the same ones that have been sold for over a century. "When we bought the business, we took a close look at all facets of it and changed a few things and added a few things. But one thing we never touched was the recipe."

So what is sponge candy all about?

"The candy itself is a unique little confection. I call it a cross between a little fluffy meringue cookie and a malted milk ball. Sweet, chocolaty,

13

Buffalo's favorite sweet treat: sponge candy! (Photo courtesy of www.fowlers chocolates.com)

and crunchy all in the same piece. It is really quite simple to make, with the center being just corn syrup, sugar, gelatin, and baking soda plus a few secret ingredients and techniques to make it our own. And then we dip them in dark chocolate, milk chocolate and orange chocolate. Sponge candy is the perfect vehicle for a perfect chocolate profile. We sell them by the thousands each year."

Fowler's is one of the few candy stores where you will find customers looking for something other than a chocolate heart for Valentine's Day. "It really is amazing. We sell a lot of sponge candy on the Fourth of July, Easter, Christmas, or just a plain old ordinary Tuesday in the middle of June. The biggest surprise, though, is Valentine's Day. People come in here not looking for hearts, but for sponge candy! It makes a great gift any time."

The one thing about Upstate candy is, well, it stays Upstate. In just this book, we meet Turkey Joints from Rome, Peppermint Pigs from Saratoga, and sponge candy from Buffalo. All three are unique in that they are virtually impossible to find anywhere in the U.S. except in these three communities and their surrounding areas. And despite their limited range, each has a strong and passionate following.

"I just got a call from a customer today," Ted told me. "He said he wanted to order a box of sponge candy to send to his father for his birthday several months down the road. He wanted to know if the candy would be ready by then," he chuckled. "I told him it was ready now. It is always ready. And I think that is important. We are reliable, and folks know they can walk through our front door and order up some sponge candy just like they have been doing for over a hundred years. If a guy calls me and says he has an aunt who used to live in Buffalo but who moved away twenty years ago to the West Coast, and she insists I get her a box of sponge candy or there will be hell to pay, well so be it. We don't want anyone to have to pay the ultimate price for not having some of our little candies!"

Fowler's makes all their own chocolates and is known for their wide variety of items, from Old World–style truffles to sea salt caramels to a wonderful little invention called TV Delite (with homemade marshmallow centers!). There are several other confectioners in the Western New York region that claim to be the home of sponge candy. But Fowler's stands by its claim as the birthplace. "As far as any research and data we have examined, we believe that our company did in fact introduce sponge candy to the world. In fact, our motto is 'Original and Authentic.'"

And that says it all!

4

SHREDDED WHEAT CEREAL
Niagara Falls

*P*oor shredded wheat.

Not always the first thing a kid thinks of every morning as he heads down to the breakfast table. But these little haystack-like bundles have been around longer than almost any other breakfast food, and they have their roots in two different Upstate New York locales.

It all starts with Henry Perky, from Denver. He was an inveterate inventor, and he came up with the notion of a cereal that would have a shelf life of forever (well, almost). In 1892 he dreamt up a way to make a dry cereal requiring no refrigeration and no pre-preparation. To bring the cereal to life, you would simply pour milk over it. The concept of a "wet" morning cereal was unheard of. He and his machinist friend William Ford of Watertown invented a machine to make these breakfast "wheat biscuits" with the idea of selling the machine, not the foods. No such luck. Customers started gobbling up the cereal as fast as it hit the shelves.

Originally the shredded wheat biscuits were sold door-to-door in Denver from a horse drawn cart. Eventually Perky settled back East and opened up a series of factories in Massachusetts and soon changed the name of his company to the simple moniker it carries even today, Shredded Wheat. In 1901, the manufacturing plant moved to Niagara Falls, and it became at that time the sole manufacturer of shredded wheat in the country.

"The factory harnessed the power of Niagara for its energy needs and quickly became a workplace role model known throughout the nation," Christopher Stoianoff told me. He is the historian for the city of Niagara

Henry Perky's quirky "wheat biscuits" now make up a large portion of the cereal options available on supermarket shelves.

Falls, New York. "The Falls provided a distinct spiritual backdrop to Perky's factory. It is such a magnetic place. He believed that the air was filled with negative ions floating all over from the pounding of the surf on the rocks. He believed that this place would clear your brain, open up one's spirituality, and that this, combined with the magnificent spectacle that is Niagara Falls, would make it an ideal location to build a workplace heretofore unseen in American business."

The factory, dubbed the Palace of Light, was way ahead of its time. It had the most modern, innovative amenities of the day: an air-conditioned work space, showers for the employees, a gymnasium and an auditorium for social gatherings, gleaming white-tiled walls, and lushly landscaped grounds. The female workers wore white dresses with frilly caps on their heads much like nurses. An immaculate dining hall offered delicious meals for the employees served to them by company chefs and waiters.

Meals were served on gold-edged china dishes and the utensils were silver. Chandeliers lit the large room, and a grand piano was situated at the front of the room for relaxing musical accompaniment. The lunches were free to the females, but the men had to pay a dime. One remarkable feature of the factory was a rooftop garden patio from which the employees could experience the mist and thunder of Niagara.

"The Palace of Light employed thousands of workers over the years," the historian told me. "I am a native of this city, and I can remember when I was a kid hearing the older folks talk wistfully about the time they spent working there. How they would bring home free, still-hot Shredded Wheat for their families at night. How they were given the first fifteen minute coffee breaks offered in America. They extolled the healthy components of the cereal and thoroughly enjoyed working there. You just never heard a bad word about the Palace of Light."

An image of this manufacturing showplace adorned the boxes of Shredded Wheat for several years. At its peak, more than one hundred thousand visitors from around the world came to the Palace of Light to tour the manufacturing area and see how Shredded Wheat was made. The tours were touted as an opportunity to see the "finest, cleanest, most hygienic food factory in the world."

Perky's "little whole wheat mattress" company (his words) was sold to National Biscuit Company (Nabisco) in 1928. The Palace of Light soon became abandoned and decrepit, and its doors were eventually closed in the 1950s.

"It was a hallmark of the era," Stoianoff lamented. "Nobody in the 1950s and 1960s saved anything having to do with history. Nobody cared about historic architecture, historic beginnings, or landmarks of the past. The wrecking ball was king. The magnificent structure that Henry Perky built as a showplace for the world was torn down in the mid-1950s. Today it is an empty field, just sitting there along the river about five blocks from Niagara Falls, waiting for a new makeover. The whole area is in the new Historic District and we believe that our city has really turned a corner and that brighter days are ahead of us. I remember the area when I was growing up. Plywood over every window, everything falling down. I am proud of the city's efforts to revitalize that area. Still, we have not much left from the glory years when Shredded Wheat and the Palace of Light were the top attractions here, along with the Falls, of course."

The story of Henry Perky's little wheat mattresses is an important one in the industrial development of Western New York. It is a difficult story to tell, however, when there is so little physical evidence of its heyday.

"As the city's historian, I am always getting questions and inquiries about our city. Only those who know of the Shredded Wheat connection ask about it. Otherwise, it never comes up. I have a few postcards with images of the Palace of Light on them. And some folks actually have yellow bricks of which the factory was constructed. 'Golden bricks,' Perky called them. People like to keep them on their mantels or as souvenirs of the old days. But I keep pumping out the fascinating stories of the company and our city's illustrious past all the while I keep celebrating our future. We only have the echoes of that great time of over a century ago, but I do my best to keep those memories alive," Stoianoff said.

Who knew shredded wheat had its beginnings in Niagara Falls? It is a great story.

Beef on Weck

Buffalo

*B*uffalo is a big-shouldered city that sits hard on the eastern shore of Lake Erie. Today it is New York's second most populated city. In 1900 it was the eighth most populated city in the whole country. Many will tell you that the city has seen its best days. Others will tell you that its brightest days are ahead of it. Regardless, Buffalo is a city of magnificent architecture, world-class parks, vibrant ethnic neighborhoods, and rabid sports fans.

And they love their food here!

Without a doubt, the Queen City is known nationally as the home of Buffalo chicken wings, and these tangy hot delicacies are dealt with in chapter 37.

In this chapter, we take a look at a unique sandwich—unique and beloved by Buffalonians since the 1800s. It is a sandwich that you can get at almost all the drink and drown saloons, all-night drive-in restaurants, fancy sit-down eateries, major ballparks, and even shopping malls. So renowned is this sandwich that it is the unofficial sandwich of Buffalo.

And yet go thirty miles past Lackawanna and most people have never heard of it.

"The Beef on Weck sandwich started here about one hundred and fifty years or so ago," Charles Roesch told me. He is the famous Charlie the Butcher in Buffalo. He is also the "King of the Beef on Weck."

"The legend goes that some German saloon owners along the water-front used to serve up pretzels and beer to their customers," Charlie told me. "Obviously they really laid on the salt because this made their patrons thirstier by the minute. Well, eventually these saloon owners decided they

Charles Roesch, Buffalo's legendary "Charlie the Butcher." (Photo courtesy of www.charliethebutcher.com)

wanted to offer something else, something a little more substantial. So they came up with a roast beef sandwich on a roll. It was something they were familiar with from the old country. Sliced cooked beef on a Kaiser roll that had been dipped in au jus. They covered the top of the roll with a coating of caraway seeds and pretzel salt to keep the customers asking for beer. They called this a kummelweck roll. *Kummel* is German for caraway. And *weck* means roll. Hence the Beef on Weck was born."

Charlie the Butcher is a legendary figure in the Buffalo area. His family name is synonymous with quality meats, going back four generations. "My grandfather started a butcher shop that my dad eventually took over," Charlie began. "The shop was in an inner city neighborhood at a place called the Broadway Market. We were there for a long time. Before long Buffalo started to grow, and by the time the shop came to me a lot of our customers were getting their beef and meats from the big chain stores in the suburbs. So I was left with a big meat case loaded with plenty of meat and no customers," he laughed.

What to do?

If there is one characteristic that Charlie is known for it is his ability to see the future, go for it, wrestle it to the ground, and emerge triumphant. "I had to make changes. One day, I was looking at all the folks walking around the Broadway Market and then looking at my full meat counter. I decided right then and there I was going to become Charlie the Butcher. A man of ideas. I put on a white hard hat and a white apron, trademarks that I still use today. I grabbed some smoked Polish sausage and shoved a stick through it. Voila! I charged a buck for it. People loved them. I stood there and watched all these people wandering around the market with my sausage on a stick and knew I had found the key to my success," he said.

Soon Charlie was experimenting with other meats. "I always knew that I would end up making sandwiches, and the Beef on Weck was a natural. It was a Buffalo landmark so I started cooking up top rounds of beef and making the kummelweck rolls. That was twenty-five years ago, and I haven't stopped since."

Charlie the Butcher is the go to man in Buffalo for this iconic sandwich. He has made thousands of them over the years. And when I say made them, I mean personally made them. "I used to go with a local TV weatherman named Tom Jolles to folks' houses and cook up the Beef on Weck right in their backyard. It was a contest. There he would be on TV giving out the weather and I would be in the background making up the sandwiches in my hard hat and white apron. I got real famous around town after that!"

Charlie has traveled the world making his beloved sandwich and introducing other cultures to Buffalo's contribution to good taste. "I have carved the Wecks everywhere—Germany, France, Moscow—just everywhere. Once I had a bet with a famous chef named Dean Fearing from Dallas. He is known as 'The Father of Southwestern Cuisine.' We are both football fans. We bet on the outcome of a Dallas Cowboys and Buffalo Bills game. Of course I lost."

So how did he pay off the wager to this famous Texan?

"I traveled to Dallas to the Mansion on Turtle Creek, one of the swankiest hotels in the world. I pulled up with my traveling oven and cooked Beef on Weck for Chef Fearing and all his Texan friends."

I asked him what the reaction was to this taste of Buffalo in Dallas. "To tell you the truth, they didn't love it," he laughed. "But they liked it a little."

Call Charlie an ambassador, and he won't give you an argument. "I have carved weck for Regis and Kathie Lee, Tim Russert, Governor Cuomo, for all the major food shows and many famous chefs. But I still get the greatest joy just serving my customers who come through my door here in Buffalo. I love this city and it has been very good to me. I have had the support of some real giants like Bob Wegman of Wegman's Supermarket and the legendary Bob Rich of Rich's Food Products here in Buffalo. Inventor Jerry Maahs has helped me by creating one of America's most popular ovens, the Alto-Shaam Cook and Hold Oven, which allows me to take my Weck on the road. My family has been beside me the whole way. In fact my son Tim will be the fourth generation in the business. I have had a great life."

So call Charlie the Butcher an ambassador if you must. But don't call him the Mayor of Buffalo.

"Heck no," the butcher told me. "That would be my grandfather."

And he is not kidding. Charles E. Roesch was mayor of Buffalo from 1930 to 1933. "Yes, he was born into the meatpacking business, then he went into politics. He ran for mayor and won, served one term, and then went back to being a butcher."

From Charlie's humble beginnings in the inner city Broadway Market to being crowned "King of the Beef on Weck," it has been a remarkable journey. You can now find his trademark sandwich at his seven different locations around Buffalo.

6

APPLE SAUSAGE
Wyoming

$\mathcal{D}$ourie's Shop Wise market has been situated at the head of this village's Main Street for more than a century. Jim Dourie bought the place when he was very young.

"I was just a kid really when we started out. My Dad had his eye on this place, and the owner wanted to retire, so Dad said to me one day, 'Jim, how about we buy that old market in town?' Well, I had no plans at the time so I said yes. We paid twenty-five thousand dollars for the whole block-long building. Just before we signed for it, I got drafted," Jim, now eighty-four, told me. "I asked the owner if he would wait for me for two years and he agreed. I took ownership of the store right after I got out of the military."

Dourie's is the only place in town to get groceries, produce, newspaper, and chitchat. Back in the beginning, Jim and his wife, Barb, decided to make breakfast sausage at the store. So they bought an old grinder and connected with local pork farmers.

"Our breakfast sausage was a big hit right away," Jim said. "People came from miles around to buy it, and the word really spread about Dourie's sausage. There were times we could hardly keep up with the demand."

"After a few years, someone suggested we flavor our sausage with apples. Wyoming County is known for its great apple production so we thought, why not?" At the time Jim and Barb's whole family was involved in this busy little store. And with the advent of their apple sausage, more help was needed.

"Boy, what a time it was back then. Nobody had ever heard of apple sausage before. We used our special blend of breakfast sausage pork and

Jim and Barb Dourie created apple sausage more than a quarter century ago. And they are still making it in Wyoming County.

just added fresh apples to it. People lined up to get it. I never left the walk-in cooler where my grinder was. I just kept making it and making it. My mother, Rosie, and my sister, Josephine, stayed up front with Barb wrapping the apple sausage just as fast as I could make it," he laughed.

Jim still spends a good deal of his time working that old grinder. "It takes me about four hours to make a forty-pound batch of apple sausage. We used to sell it just fresh but after a while we decided to make it and freeze it so folks could get it all year long." Jim's sons, Joseph and John, help out, especially when it gets busy.

"We decided to have a little fun with our sausage so we came up with the idea to introduce a new flavored sausage just about every year. After the apple, we made maple sausage, and then many other flavors followed. Now we have pumpkin, pineapple, elderberry, chorizo, sundried tomato, buttermilk, and many more flavors. And there isn't a clunker in the bunch," Jim said.

Wyoming is a beautiful little community with much history. One of the real charms of it is that Wyoming is the last remaining village in New

York to be lit by gas. The village sits on a large natural gas deposit, and for as long as anyone can remember the old-fashioned lamps up and down the streets have flickered with the light of natural gas in the evening. It really gives the town a patina of nineteenth-century quaintness and charm.

"Yup, they call us the Gaslight Village," Jim remarked.

They also hold a doozie of a festival every year.

"Every September we have what we call our AppleUmpkin Festival," Jim said. "It started out as a way to showcase our apple and pumpkin harvests. Now, it is one of the largest festivals in the area. Nearly ten thousand come to the event, which takes place on the closed off Main Street right in front of our market."

I asked Jim if that was a hectic day or not at Dourie's Shop Wise.

"Oh, good lord is it ever. We open up the back door of the store and people are lined up in the parking lot, straight through the store, up to the cash register, and out to the festival. We stock up on all of our flavored sausages for that day, but we always run out at the end. We sell hundreds of pounds of it, and most of it is our good old apple sausage. It is a great day, and we see many old friends who have moved out of the area and come home for AppleUmpkin."

I wanted to know, after sixty years, what is the future of his store?

"Well, Barb and I are going to stay right here as long as we can. We love Wyoming, and the people around here have been so wonderful to us. I just can't imagine living anywhere else. It is just about perfect here."

I asked Barb if she had decided on the newest flavored sausage for the coming year. She just waved her hands and strode away.

"Well, we all have our favorites around here, so picking the newest flavor can get a bit touchy," Jim laughed.

Region Three

FINGER LAKES

*Monroe, Livingston, Steuben, Cayuga, Wayne, Ontario, Yates,
Schuyler, Seneca, Tioga, Onondaga, Cortland, Tompkins*

7

GARBAGE PLATE

Rochester

For a dish so inelegantly named, the Garbage Plate at Nick Tahou's place is actually quite delicious.

On a recent visit to this downtown landmark, I was surprised at how many variations of the original Garbage Plate there are. When I visited Nick Tahou Hots several years ago, the menu offered just the original. It consisted of a plate of macaroni salad piled on with hash brown potatoes, gravy, baked beans, chili, and whatever else the grill cook had handy. Now you can order the hungry man's favorite late-night dinner in combinations including egg, grilled cheese, fried ham, chicken, sausage, cheeseburger, and even a veggie garbage plate.

Alex Tahou founded the restaurant in 1918, and he was succeeded by his son, Nicolao, who ran it for more than fifty years until his death in 1997. The founder's grandson, also named Alex, continues the family tradition today. The restaurant is located in a large red brick warehouse just on the fringe of Rochester's downtown business district. The 1881 building was once the main terminal for the Buffalo, Rochester and Pittsburgh Railway. The huge structure is empty now except for Nick Tahou's on the ground floor.

The restaurant serves all the usual diner fare, including sandwiches, meals, breakfasts, and homemade soups and chili. But, let's face it. It is all about the Garbage Plate here. On the day I last visited, a long line of customers snaked their way up to the counter where the regulars would shout out their desires. "One original, no chili," or "a hots and potatoes, no

Two Garbage Plates with the works at Nick Tahou's in Rochester.

mac," or even "an original, heavy." That, I found out later, was a Garbage Plate with an extra dose of everything.

Nick Tahou's signature dish is perhaps the one item in this whole book that has reached mythic legend status. Business men, medical professionals, moms with young families, and tourists flock to this low profile eatery all day long. A sign proclaims it as "The Home of the Garbage Plate," but that sign hangs up near the roof of the towering old railroad terminal. If you are walking down the sidewalk you would never guess what kind of dining rarity awaits you inside the dark windows along the front.

Nick Tahou was a legendary character himself and was generous with his Garbage Plate profits. He also knew a good thing when he had it. The term Garbage Plate is trademarked by this single restaurant, leaving all the others in the Rochester area trying to glom on with dishes called the "sloppy plate," "junk plate", "trash plate," and even "kitty litter plate." Pretenders to the throne all.

All of the food channels and shows have pulled up to Nick Tahou's to film the making of a Garbage Plate. The Travel Channel's *Chowdown*

Countdown, Adam Richman and his *Man v. Food* series, and the Food Network's *Best Thing I Ever Ate* series have all filmed here.

One of the most bizarre pop culture events I ever found in researching this book concerns a cemetery. Rochester's main cemetery is Mount Hope. Among the luminaries buried here are Frederick Douglass, Susan B. Anthony, inventors, politicians, entertainers, and writers.

And Nick Tahou.

For many years, students at Rochester Institute of Technology have celebrated Nick's birthday by stopping by the restaurant, picking up a Garbage Plate, and heading out to Mount Hope Cemetery to enjoy it while sitting at Nick's grave.

So if you are around on January 10, well, now you know the drill.

GRAPE PIE
Naples

*M*any consider Monica Schenk to be royalty out here in the Finger Lakes.

"Yes," she chuckled, "somewhere along the line they dubbed me the Grape Pie Queen."

Monica's Pie Shop, located just north of the pretty little village of Naples, is a small, compact retail store and bakery. Everything is purple here, in honor of the region's famous grapes. "Yes, we have purple flags, banners, carpet, paint, and everything. Even the village's fire hydrants are painted purple. I'll bet you have never seen that before," she said.

Many of the Finger Lake's leading vintners can be found within a short drive of here, and there are beautiful vineyards that pop up along the roadsides and undulate slowly off into the distance. Canandaigua Lake makes for a stunning backdrop to this "Tuscany of the Finger Lakes."

So what the heck is a grape pie?

"Well, it all started years ago. I married into the grape growing business. Back in 1983 my husband, Gregory, had a big leftover crop of blues. I mean the blue grapes, Concords, which just weren't selling. White wine was all the rage back then so we had all these left over blue grapes that he wanted to just throw out. I said, 'Let me try something.' My mother, Katherine Clark, had an old grape pie recipe that we tried out. Not many had even heard of that kind of pie before. So she and I made up a batch and put them out on a road stand in front of our farm. We just left a box for money out there on a picnic table. It was all on the honor system back then."

So how did the sales of this new and mysterious pie go?

32

Monica Schenk, the Grape Pie Queen of Naples, New York.

"After a while, I went out and checked, and they were all gone," she laughed. "And it went on like that for a while until we started this little business."

Little is the definition of understatement.

Monica's Pie Shop now makes grape pies for all occasions. Big ones, little ones, different crusts, all kinds. She still bakes everything herself, right in the basement of the shop. While I was visiting with this cheerful baker in her shop kitchen, you could hear the bell on the front door chiming time after time signaling another happy customer was upstairs picking up a pie. It was nonstop.

"We sell about fifteen thousand pies a year. I get my grapes all from local farmers, too. The process was real hit-and-miss in the beginning. Making a grape pie can be messy. But eventually I found the secret. We make our crusts first and then fill them with the grapes and bake them all together. This keeps our pie crusts dry and crunchy. People like that, I guess."

I asked Monica if she sells online or in catalog.

"No," was her firm answer. "We did once and it's a funny story. I got a call in 2002 from the television Food Network. They had heard of the Grape Pie Queen of Naples and wanted to come and film me in my shop. I said that was fine, but they told me I had to have mail order available since it was a national television show. I didn't. So I took a month to get it together with phone lines, boxes, UPS slips, labels, the whole bit. They came and filmed, and it was so much fun. The whole town was excited.

"Well, on the day of the show we all gathered down here in the shop to watch it. Everybody—family, friends, workers. It was a great segment, and we all cheered when it was over. And then it happened."

"What?" I asked.

"Within three seconds after the show went off, our phones started ringing with mail orders. Every phone. We were running around down here like chickens with our heads cut off. Writing down orders on slips of papers. It was just unbelievable. We just had no idea what we were getting ourselves into. We took hundreds of orders. We had signed a contract with the Food Network that we would have mail order available for as long as the show ran. That was five years. When the show *Food Finds* finally got cancelled I stopped taking mail orders the very next day! It was way too much work and it was very expensive to do. So, no mail orders anymore. If you want a Monica's Grape Pie you have to come to Naples. But I have to admit, being on television was pretty cool!" she said.

Monica's continues to be a family affair. "My kids all started here when they were tiny. In fact, my youngest, Joseph, was in here at about a year old banging on the kitchen windows while we were trying to take orders. And my mom, the original Queen, is still my right hand assistant. She is ninety-five years old now and I call her 'my crust lady.'"

Monica is always on the lookout for the next big thing. Her shop is loaded with grape- and wine-themed novelties and gifts. She continues to add items to her expanding menu, too. "We just started making chicken pot pies. We can hardly keep them in stock," she told me as she brushed pie crust off her purple apron.

Recently Monica signed an agreement with the Pfaltzgraff Company, a leading maker of kitchenware, to be their "pie expert" and to help them create the perfect pie plate.

Naples is a lovely little Finger Lakes village. They hold a Grape Festival every September that attracts thousands of visitors. You can find many places that sell grape pies here. I was a newcomer to it all when I arrived to spend the afternoon with Monica. Not only had I never tasted a grape pie before, but I had never heard of it. You can bet that I went home with one, though. Monica packed up a fresh pie and some jams and breads for me in her ubiquitous neon purple shopping bags, and off I went like a Johnny Appleseed spreading the word of the lost art of grape pie making.

"I just love it here. I work seven days a week, every day of the year. We are one of the only ones who stay open daily during the hard winters we get Upstate. I love chatting with my customers, some of whom have been coming in here since I opened up. I still chuckle when people come in and ask if the Queen is here. Even the *New York Times* came and did an interview with me. But, that is all fine and good with me. As long as folks are happy and enjoy my grape pies, well, then 'long live the Queen,'" she said with a big smile.

9

SALT POTATOES

Syracuse

*S*alt potatoes. Salt plus potatoes. Simple.

Salt potatoes are unique to the Syracuse area. Known as the Salt City, Syracuse was at one time the leading salt manufacturer in the country. Natural salt mines dotted the perimeter of Onondaga Lake, and the salt industry sprouted up for miles all along the lake. The process of "solar drying" the salt from the briny water was a huge endeavor. Large beds of wet salty water were laid out side by side for as far as the eye could see, drying in the afternoon sun. Thousands of workers in the industry toiled daily, stirring the brine, covering it with miniature pyramids when lake storms blew over it, and then packing it up and onto barges along the Erie Canal and, later, the railroads.

Eventually huge cooking pots took the place of the sun as thousands of gallons of salty lake water was channeled into salt houses around the lake where the salt was boiled down to its solid state. It was hard, dirty and dangerous work. Today, a Salt Museum on the northern shore of Onondaga Lake in Liverpool gives testimony to the importance of the salt industry to the growth of Syracuse in the 1800s.

A salt potato was a poor man's delicacy during the building of the Erie Canal. Using small white potatoes, canal workers would soak these round spuds in the naturally salty water of the lake and then boil them over an open fire. They were the mainstay of the diets of these laborers, many of whom were immigrants. Because salty water boils at a higher temperature, the resulting potato is much creamier than a nonsalted potato.

John Hinerwadel put Syracuse's salt potato on the map more than a century ago. His family still sells thousands of bags of them annually.

It wasn't long before a sharp entrepreneur would come along and mass produce and mass market this popular dinner, picnic, and clambake side dish. John Hinerwadel got the notion that one need not have the convenience of living lakeside in Syracuse to enjoy salt potatoes. In the early part of the twentieth century, he began packaging up his potatoes in a five-pound bag, which included a packet of Syracuse salt in it! This catchy innovation spread the word of Syracuse's little potato favorites far and wide, and his family business, still going strong more than a century later, now sells thousands of five-pound bags of salt potatoes each year.

The Hinerwadel family owns a sprawling, campus-like facility just north of Syracuse where they host thousands of people annually at corporate picnics, weddings, reunions, and public gatherings. The grounds are meticulously landscaped and are particularly spectacular in the spring and early summer. Of course, during the catering negotiations with each individual group, Hinerwadel's salt potatoes are always suggested as a menu item.

Hinerwadel's Grove consists of more than thirty acres of grounds and can handle several different functions at the same time. Groups as large as three thousand can be accommodated. The family venue, known as "Central New York's Original Clambake Facility," has been holding these outdoor repasts here since 1914. In the early days of the business, Hinerwadel's Grove was so popular that a train line was established to bring city dwellers out to these clambakes, just a couple of miles from downtown Syracuse.

Now in the hands of the fourth generation of Hinerwadels, it continues to be one of the most popular outdoor venues in Central New York. While here, visitors can also see the hundreds of crates piled high with salt potatoes, as well as purchase some at the shop. The iconic white paper bag declares in bright red letters "Hinerwadel's Famous Original Salt Potatoes" with a classic red and yellow beaming sun behind it.

10

MEATBALLS IN A HEEL

Syracuse

*T*he Columbus Baking Company looks like a movie set from an old Italian film. Cement floors, old work stations, high ceilings, two ancient ovens roaring away in the back. Bakers with T-shirts and white aprons shoveling loaves into the fire-breathing monsters a dozen at a time using long handled wooden peels. Flour everywhere. Mixers churning dough. An old wooden bench with even older men sitting on it out front. The air filled with the lilting sounds of a faraway language. A real Old World Italian bakery.

"Yeah, but wait a minute. I'm Greek," Jimmy Retzos Sr. told me with a laugh. "My grandfather, Angelo, came over from Greece in 1926. This Italian bakery had already been open for thirty years. He couldn't speak a word of Italian, but he was a hard worker, so they hired him. There were seven original Italian partners in the bakery. Over the years as they retired and passed on, my grandfather, then my dad, and then myself all bought into the business. We have been open here on Pearl Street for 117 years."

The Columbus Baking Company is one of Syracuse's real treasures. There is absolutely nothing fancy about this place. It is plain, it is simple and it is old.

"Hey, it's just bread. Four ingredients. Water, flour, yeast and salt," the owner told me. "Simple. But we make it the same way it's always been made here. And that means a lot to our customers. We are a tradition. Nothing changes here. Even our two ovens are over a hundred years old. They started as wood burning, then coal, and now gas. You know what

Deli manager Shannon Retzos displays her artistry in making a hundred Meatball in a Heel sandwiches a day!

you are going to get when you walk in the front door of Columbus. Nothing changes. Still the best bread in Syracuse."

The ovens get fired up at three in the morning. When they are ready, each one welcomes 350 loaves when fully loaded. Jimmy Jr. is usually here at that time of the day overseeing things. He will be the fourth generation Retzos when the time comes for him to put on the master baker's apron.

Several years back, the bakery opened up a deli in an adjoining storefront. Daughter-in-law Shannon runs that side of the business. "It was overwhelming at first but I really enjoy it now," she told me. "We sell several different kinds of sandwiches, all on our own bread of course. And our most popular item is the Meatballs in a Heel."

I asked Jimmy Sr. where the idea for this sandwich originated. "In the olden days we used to deliver our bread to all the bars and restaurants in the city. Late at night. Well, we found out the bars would take our bread, hollow it out and stuff it with meatballs or sausages. Every bar used to do this. Not anymore, though. So when we opened up our deli we decided to bring this tradition back to the city. It is hugely popular."

I asked Shannon to make me up "a heel" to take with me. She cut a loaf of pointy bread in half (they make a round-ended Italian loaf and a pointy-ended one). She then hollowed it out. Next she stuffed it to overflowing with meatballs (I counted nine when I was eating it later), drizzled some spaghetti sauce over and into it, and then layered mozzarella cheese slices over the top. The final touch is placing all the "stuffing"—the bread she took out of the loaf—over the top. "People insist on having it to dip into the sauce," she told me.

It really was delicious. And easy to eat. Unlike a meatball sub sandwich, which flops all over when you are trying to walk with it, the heel holds the contents in a rigged natural container. I suggested to Shannon this would be a great fair item.

"You are right. In fact take a look at what's outside in the lot," she said.

I jumped out and took a glimpse into the parking spot next to the bakery. There I saw a new, gleaming, portable food truck. "We go to all the fairs, festivals, sporting events, parades, everything around the area. We usually take just a couple of our items with us. We take a chicken parm heel, some pizza frites, which are strips of our bread deep fried with sugar on them, and of course our meatball heel. By far and away it is the number one item we sell in the deli and on the road."

Shannon was getting ready for the lunch crowd as I began to leave. "Look up here," she pointed. There on the kitchen wall was a quantity of slips of preordered Meatballs in a Heel. Some were for a few, others were for a dozen. "It's going to be a busy lunch hour," she smiled.

The owner told me there is a lot of history inside his simple old bakery. "All the generations of my family worked here over these same ovens. It means a lot to me. People come back year after year. If they have moved away and come back for a wedding or a funeral or something, they always come back to see if we are still here."

A lot of sports stars, politicians, and entertainers have come through Syracuse over the years. I asked him if they ever made it down to the bakery.

"Oh, sure," he replied. "In fact President Jimmy Carter was here in Syracuse in 1980. I think he was speaking at Syracuse University or something. Anyways, his motorcade was coming down I-81 and one of his Secret Service agents must have been from around here, so he suggested the president go down to the bakery and get some bread. All of a sudden here comes the whole presidential entourage right here on little Pearl Street. Several big guys came in with expensive suits and sunglasses and earpieces and the whole bit. They bought five loaves of bread and went back to their cars and sped off."

"Did the president come into the bakery?" I asked.

"No he didn't. But about a half an hour later the bakery phone rang. My father answered it. 'Columbus Bakery,' he shouted into the speaker. The man on the other end asked for George Retzos. My father said, 'Speaking.' The other voice said, 'George, this is President Jimmy Carter. I am on Air Force One at Syracuse Airport right this minute eating your bread. It is the best Italian bread I have ever had and I just wanted to tell you to never stop making it.'"

I asked him what his father's reaction was to the presidential phone call.

"I was standing right next to him. We heard a long silence as my dad was listening to the president. When the president stopped talking my dad said, 'Thanks,' hung up the phone, and went back to the ovens!"

11

CORNELL CHICKEN

Syracuse

$\mathcal{B}$ob Baker never met a chicken he didn't like. Whole, cut up, broiled, fricasseed, roasted it didn't matter. He had an undying, scholarly passion for poultry. But when a unique invention came along, Dr. Baker really went into overdrive.

"My Dad actually had a hand in creating one of the first chicken deboning machines," Reenie Standsted told me. She is Bob Baker's daughter. "Once he was able to get the bone out of the chicken he really went to town. He studied poultry for years at Cornell University, and he was tasked with coming up with new ways to serve chicken, the whole chicken, including parts that had never been used before. Coming up with that machine really made a difference in dad's work."

Dr. Robert Baker (1921–2006) chaired Cornell's Department of Poultry and Avian Sciences. In 1970, he founded the university's Institute of Food Science and Marketing. His interest was world hunger and food science, and he traveled extensively around the globe exploring ways to feed the hungry. Poultry was his forte. He was deeply interested in how people thought of chicken, and he worked tirelessly on methods to alter the way we eat it. He wrote nearly three hundred scholarly papers on the subject. Academically speaking, Dr. Baker was a pioneer. He was inducted into the American Poultry Hall of Fame. He retired from Cornell as professor emeritus in 1989.

However, if you think Dr. Baker was a white lab-coated statistician checking on petri dishes and test tubes all day long, well, you are wrong. Bob Baker was a lively and personable man who loved to invent new food items. More than forty food innovations are credited to Dr. Baker, not the

43

Cornell chicken has been a State Fair tradition since 1949. Everyone from governors to movie stars and even U.S. presidents have eaten at Bob Baker's Chicken Coop.

least being the chicken nugget! He invented this item a quarter century before McDonald's glommed on to it and crowned the new item Chicken McNuggets.

"My father was an innovator," Reenie told me. "He invented chicken baloney, chicken hot dogs, and many other items including the chicken nugget."

"Did he make a lot of money with this invention?" I asked.

"No. He did it all for Cornell. It was his life's work. Again, once the deboning machine came along the possibilities for chicken were endless. And that is where the nuggets came from. Of course years later when he started seeing McDonald's and all the other places selling chicken nuggets he would just smile. He was very proud of his work, but no, he didn't make any money from that creation. He was just honored to have invented it."

Her father must have been quite the whiz in the kitchen, I surmised.

"No," was the firm answer. "My mom, Jacoba, was the cook in our house, not Dad," she said. Jackie is now ninety-three.

A longstanding tribute to Dr. Baker's efforts on behalf of the lowly chicken can still be seen every year at the New York State Fair in Syracuse. For more than sixty years fairgoers have been flocking to Baker's Chicken Coop for some mouthwatering barbecue chicken. The stand was founded by Dr. Baker to highlight his innovation known as Cornell chicken.

"Cornell chicken actually started at Penn State in the 1940s where he was teaching. Dad and two partners came to Cornell in 1948 and just gave it to the school. Up until that time nobody was cooking chickens outside on a grill. It was just unheard of. My father did a lot of research on the subject of grilling. How to position the rack, how to place the charcoals or wood for burning, when to turn the chickens, how to get the right heat under them, and how to construct a pit that was large enough.

"Anybody that was grilling in those days was basting their chicken with a thick red sauce. This usually burned and made a terrible mess. Dad came up with his own sauce that was thinner, tastier, and didn't burn. The recipe is fairly simple. So when I say he gave it to Cornell, he gave not so much the recipe for the chicken but rather the whole concept and technique of how to grill it properly on an outdoor rack that would hold fifty chickens at once. I know it sounds kind of ordinary now, but Dad actually wrote a manual on all this and published it in the *Cornell Bulletin* more than fifty years ago."

Baker's Chicken Coop is still run by the Baker family.

"Dad just wanted to let as many people as possible know about his 'famous' chicken so he opened up this little eatery at the Fair in 1949. It was originally just a tent. His partners quickly gave up, and it became a family run business. My parents had six kids and we all grew up at the Chicken Coop. The minute my mom thought we were old enough to work there, we did. It's a wonderful experience when you are twelve years old to spend your summers at the New York State Fair," she remembered. "Oh, my, the times we had."

Today, Reenie and her three sisters Karen, Regina, and Johanna run it.

I asked if there was ever a moment at the Chicken Coop that really stood out for her.

"Well, when Hillary Clinton was beginning in politics in 1999 she went on a 'listening tour' of New York State. I was invited to meet her at Cornell

University. She was so warm and friendly that I invited her to the New York State Fair to discuss horticulture, which is my passion. She wrote me later and said she wanted to come visit us at the Fair and could she bring her husband with her. I mean, she asked if she could bring the president of the United States with her to our Chicken Coop. Imagine," she said.

"They came and we had a ball. They loved Dad's Cornell Chicken and ate it right at our picnic table at the stand. I have never seen my father more proud than he was that day."

Dr. Baker and his wife also founded Baker's Acres in North Lansing just up the road from his beloved Cornell University. Reenie now owns it and it is one of the largest herb and perennial growers in Central New York. She gives many classes at her garden center to help her customers develop green thumbs.

In parting I asked Reenie what it was like growing up with her famous dad.

"He was a serious man but a fun man. Very humble. And, since he had so many kids, we were his tasting board. So I guess you could say we got to eat a chicken nugget before anybody else. It was pretty cool."

Did she like all of her dad's food creations?

"Well, there was something called creamy fish bites he had us try once. Yuck!" she laughed.

And so while our downstate friends are tripping all over each other to grab the latest little morsel from Momofuku's gourmet table or maybe the latest tidbit from the kitchen of star chef Maguy Le Coze's Le Bernardin, we will tip our rural toques to the genius that was Dr. Robert Baker, the Thomas Edison of Poultry.

Dr. Baker's Cornell Chicken (Marinade) Sauce (Recipe)

1 egg
1 cup vegetable oil
2 cups cider vinegar
3 tablespoons coarse salt
1 tablespoon poultry seasoning
½ teaspoon freshly ground black pepper

Beat the egg, add oil, beat again.
Add remaining ingredients and stir.
Use the sauce for basting.
While barbecuing, brush sauce on chicken each time you turn it.
Makes enough sauce for 10 halves.

Region Four

THOUSAND ISLANDS/SEAWAY

Oswego, Jefferson, St. Lawrence

12

GRANDMA BROWN'S
HOME BAKED BEANS
Mexico

*O*ne of Upstate New York's most familiar food icons is a little old lady with white curly hair and crinkly eyes peering out at you from the label on a can of beans. The color of the can, kind of an off color yellow that fades to washed-out brown, hasn't been tinkered with for a half century. The only graphic on the can is a big old bright red sloppy pan of baked beans. Oh, and the baked beans come from Mexico.

That's Grandma Brown's Home Baked Beans, an Upstate food legend. Let me explain.

People have been buying this no-frills side dish ever since the original Grandma Brown started peddling her homemade beans in stores around her community of Mexico, New York, back around the Great Depression. With very few changes, this food favorite continues today with a new generation of Browns operating out of a factory still located in Mexico.

The company prides itself on being old fashioned. The label remains the same, and the image of Grandma is the same as ever. Still old, but never aging. The ingredients have never changed, there are still no chemicals added to them. The baked beans are naturally gluten free and low in fat, contain no preservatives, and are high in potassium. In fact, the ingredient list on the can names only five items to make this legendary product. And one of those is water.

The company has no website, employs almost no fan outreach, and is reluctant to submit to the encroachment of the modern social media maelstrom. They are old fashioned, darn it, and they intend to stay that way.

Everything about Grandma Brown's Home Baked Beans has stayed the same throughout the years, even the famous brown, yellow, and red label.

It is very hard to find even the phone number of the manufacturing plant in Mexico. After some moments of early frustration, I finally found the number in the most likely of places: right on the can! I called them for an interview for this book and spoke with a Mrs. Brown (yes, she told me she is a descendent of the original Grandma). Although she was very polite, she remained tight-lipped when it came to talking to me about her company. When I asked if we could meet for an interview someday, she told me she would think about it and get back to me.

She never did. And that is okay with me.

I went to Mexico to check out this mysterious food legend firsthand. The company is housed in a low-slung, baked bean–colored building. The identification sign reflects the simpler times and plain business credo of its origins. No flashy neon marquee. No animated dancing baked beans. No digitalized welcome billboard. Just an ordinary sign across the front that says, "This Is Where Grandma Brown's Baked Beans Are Made."

Although simple and quaint in its antiquity (the actual cooking in-structions on the label basically say open the can, pour into dish, and heat), the company does a whale of a business. Grandma Brown's Home Baked Beans are sold in all the major supermarkets in the Upstate region. They are a staple to folks here, and those who were brought up on Grandma Brown's creation have taken that love far and wide when the urge to leave Mexico sends them forth. People from around the country, former Upstaters, still crave the taste of Mexico's pride and joy, and they bombard the company with orders from the four corners of the USA. And these customers are dogged. The company has no website, no emails, no Twitter, no hash tags, and no URLs. And they do not accept credit cards, so you have to mail them a check or money order when you order (you remember mail, don't you?).

There is a Facebook page for Granny, but I doubt if the company authorized it. Maybe, though. The last time I checked it hadn't been updated in over a year. Like I said, old fashioned.

There are just a few products in Grandma Brown's official family, mainly the beans and some soups. The beans come in several mostly standard sizes. There is one size, however, that is sure to be a head-turner at your next family picnic. The giant family sized can weighs in at a whopping fifty-four ounces! That is more than three pounds of pure, homespun, delectable Upstate goodness!

We who live in Upstate New York are lucky to have Grandma Brown's Home Baked Beans as near as the neighborhood supermarket. For those who have wandered far from our friendly confines, it is tricky trying to fulfill your longing for some of the best baked beans east of the Mississippi. But there is one way to satisfy your desire: Granny's beans may be one of the only items from this book that you can actually buy on eBay!

13

THOUSAND ISLAND DRESSING

Clayton

*I*n a recent poll by the Food Network, America was asked, "What is your favorite salad dressing?" Thousand Island dressing didn't even come near the top.

Oh, the glories of the vaunted buttermilky ranch dressing, the choice of the most voters. And "all hail Caesar" and the familial triumvirate of dressings descending from vinaigrette to Caesar to Italian. And coming in at the number five spot is fancy and snooty bleu cheese dressing, which we all know is really more of a dip than a dressing. But enough of the semantics.

Even though Thousand Island dressing doesn't even achieve runner-up status here, it does have its fans, fanatics, and worshippers. Especially in Upstate New York.

While surely every New Yorker knows that our state gem is the ruby garnet, our state bug is the nine-spotted ladybug, and our state shell is the bay scallop, how many can name the official New York State salad dressing? Well, nobody can because there isn't one. But if they ever solicit nominations, you would be hard pressed to find a more perfect born-in-New York salad topper than Thousand Island dressing.

Its origins can be found near where "the river meets the lake." Clayton is a village of five thousand, situated on the St. Lawrence Seaway in far northern Jefferson County. In this land of natural beauty, ancient lighthouses, and local conversations tinged with enough continental lilt to make even the most hardened Francophone wistful, you will find the nostalgic Thousand Islands Inn, birthplace of the eponymous dressing.

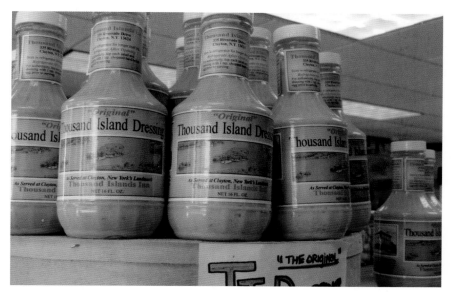

Thousand Island dressing, made with the original recipe, can be bought online or at the Thousand Islands Inn in Clayton.

Established in 1897, this hotel is one of the last ones standing from an age when opulence was the operative word here, when the rich and famous came to the cool waters of the St. Lawrence River far from the muggy confines of midtown Manhattan. The names of those who settled here (seasonally, of course) read like a page out of Mrs. Astor's and Mrs. Vanderbilt's famous blue books of social registry: George Pullman, who made traveling palaces called Pullman Sleeping Cars, in which the well-heeled traversed the rails; Louis Marx, an American-born multimillionaire Cuban sugar baron; Nathan Straus and Abraham Abraham, who together owned Macy's and Abraham & Straus department stores, and who lived here on Cherry Island in twin castles; and Commodore Frederick Bourne, onetime head of the Singer Sewing Machine Company, whose fortress home in the seaway was once known as Dark Castle and now goes by the more apt name of Singer Castle.

And let's not forget the most famous castle keeper of them all along the seaway, George Boldt. He owned several hotels and was internationally famous as the general manager of New York City's ritzy Waldorf Astoria (which itself, for those interested, gave us the Waldorf salad in 1895).

The story of Boldt Castle is one of the most poignant and oft told tales of the region. Boldt built his showplace on Heart Island near the international water boundary between the United States and Canada. He wanted to present his wife with "the most opulent private residence" in the country. Sadly, Louise K. Boldt died in 1904, before her husband's magnum opus was finished. A distraught George walked away from the half-finished castle and never looked back. For seven decades it sat deteriorating in the middle of the St. Lawrence, a sad token to a love story aborted. Today the castle, which has been renovated over the years, is one of the top tourist destinations in the region.

OK, back to the dressing.

Fishing guide George LaLonde and his wife, Sophia, concocted the first generation of the famous salad goop while serving rich guests on fishing escapades around the seaway. The simple recipe has changed very little over the last century or so. With its mixture of ketchup, pickle relish, and mayonnaise (plus seasoned to taste), the plain and simple three-ingredient condiment seemed hardly destined for greatness.

One time the celebrated actress May Irwin and her husband visited the area and hired the LaLondes as their hosts. Irwin was a vaudevillian star, an acclaimed "white coon shouter" who sang African American standards to standing room–only crowds around the country. She was fabulously wealthy, making as much as $2,500 per week while still in her twenties. Her lasting claim to fame is that Thomas Edison filmed her with actor John C. Rice performing the first-ever movie kiss in 1896.

The influential Irwin fell in love with the LaLondes' tangy and unusual-looking salad dressing, which was served at the Herald House in Clayton. She eventually brought word of her newfound delicacy back to New York City and told her friend and fellow seaway visitor Boldt about it. He quickly put it on the menu of his tony Waldorf Astoria. When he asked Miss Irwin what the name of the salad dressing was, she replied, "Thousand Island dressing."

May Irwin eventually became a resident of the region herself, purchasing a mansion on Grindstone Island. She later owned a farm in

Clayton. Susan and Allen Benas purchased the property, known as the Herald Hotel, in 1972 and christened the grand old lady from another era the Thousand Islands Inn.

Over the years many celebrities of all stripes have stayed or dined at the inn. I am sure they all had Thousand Island dressing on their salad. From Admiral Richard Byrd, discoverer of the South Pole, to Country Music Hall-of-Famer Johnny Cash to Baseball Hall-of-Famer Warren Spahn, everybody and anybody who has come through the seaway's outdoor playground has stopped by.

The inn's owners still sell the famous dressing in limited quantities, using the original recipe. They make only five thousand bottles of it annually, and they sell it during business hours from May through September. It is also available, slathered on salads of course, in the main dining room.

There are naysayers and conspiracy theorists who will challenge the birthplace of this pinkish, chunky salad-bar staple. But Allen Benas swears it was "born" at his inn. He will tell any eager myth debunker that he found the original disintegrating recipe in the safe of the hotel when he bought the place and that nobody knows the recipe except for his chef, his wife, and himself.

The Thousand Islands Inn has been featured in many newspaper articles, food columns, and television programs, including CBS's *Sunday Morning*. It is listed on the National Registry of Historic Places.

14

TOM AND JERRY COCKTAIL
Watertown

*I*n this chapter I make the sole departure from Upstate *foods* to Upstate *drinks*. I suppose I could have waxed on and on about the joys of different Upstate beverages, but I wanted this book to be about foods only.

Residents of Buffalo will no doubt swoon at the mere mention of Loganberry soda, a fruit-flavored soft drink found almost nowhere other than Erie County. Beer drinkers around the country have a jolly old time deriding the heady taste of a Genny Cream Ale. Locals will merely smile with pride that their beloved "screamers" won back-to-back gold medals at the Great American Beer Festival. At Hustler's Tavern in Lewiston, they used to serve a "gin mixture that would warm the body and soul and was worthy to be served in vessels of diamonds." In the early 1800s, the barmaid, Catherine Hustler, stuck roosters' tails in her gin drinks and American soldiers first dubbed them cocktails. And snatch away somebody's dark-blue bottle of Saratoga Spring Water, bottled there since 1872, and you can prepare yourself for some Revolutionary fireworks!

Yes, they are all beloved Upstate beverages (and there are many more, of course): a Buffalo soft drink, a Rochester beer icon, pure and sweet water at the foothills of the Adirondacks, and Lewiston, the birthplace of the cocktail. Surely, I could do a whole chapter on beverages.

But let's talk about the Tom and Jerry for a moment.

"People start talking about getting their Tom and Jerrys around the first snowfall up here," Libby DePhtereos told me. My visit with the young and energetic owner of the famous Crystal Bar and Restaurant on the square in downtown Watertown took place during a busy weekday lunch

58

Owners Peter and Libby Dephtereos hold the original eighty-year-old Tom and Jerry bowl still used today.

hour. The restaurant and bar, the oldest in Watertown, was a bustle of activity.

"Folks have been coming in here for generations," Libby told me. "My husband's grandfather started it and it has been in the same family for over eighty years."

The old wooden booths sparkle more with age than with gloss. The booth benches bend with your body, making them comfortable and hard to leave. The pressed-tin ceiling has a million stories to tell, and the floor tiles, hand laid nearly a century ago, echo the tramp of mothers and children and office workers and soldiers stopping by for a generous plate of homemade food at a wallet-friendly price.

"I love this place for the joy it brings so many people," the owner said. "We see friends who have been meeting here for a cup of coffee for years. It is a familiar gathering place in the downtown area where people come to eat and get all the gossip. We never change the décor, which is original to about 1919. People like that. It is a real throwback to yesterday, or to what many of our customers call 'the good old days.' We even have a waitress who has been working here for over fifty years!"

The front space of the Crystal is taken up by a large oak bar. "It is the last stand-up bar in New York. No stools. There never have been any. The original owner thought that if you have had too much to drink to be able to stand up then it is time to go. There is a lot of history in that old stand up bar," she said wistfully.

It is at the ancient Crystal bar that something magical happens every holiday season. "My husband's grandfather, who came from Greece, started a tradition of serving a Tom and Jerry cocktail during the Christmas season. Actually many of the working men's bars in the North Country did this. The Crystal is the last one to continue the tradition. Right after Thanksgiving they would bring out a very old bowl that they got many years ago from the Woodruff Hotel, which is now gone. People would start coming in for a mug of Tom and Jerry to celebrate the holidays with their friends. They still do. People actually come from miles around for it.

"This place gets packed every day from Thanksgiving to New Year's. The bowl is on the bar and we make each Tom and Jerry to order. Sometimes the girls in the back are making thirty or forty at a time. The magic really does happen back there in the kitchen," she laughed. "Nobody sees the drink being made, and when it comes out to the bar everybody cheers. It is nonstop and it is a madhouse in here. A fun madhouse though."

I asked Libby for the Tom and Jerry recipe. "Well, after you warm up the individual mug you put in our special mixtures and rum and brandy and some spices and you have a Tom and Jerry." I chuckled as I quizzed her about the recipe, suggesting that she deliberately left some ingredients out. "To tell you the truth, I can't tell you the recipe. If I did I would have to kill you and then shoot myself," she said with a dainty smile.

I told Libby and her husband, Pete, that I thought this was one of the most charming holiday traditions I have run across in researching this book. "People will not let us stop it. And we don't want to. Like I said, just before Thanksgiving we start getting calls asking us if it's Tom and Jerry time yet. It gives everybody something to look forward to. And something to share with friends. It is a part of the holidays here in Watertown, where the winters can be long and cold. They just can't wait to come into this old place and warm up with a real tradition from days gone by, our Tom and Jerry."

I asked Libby whether she still uses the old original bowl from the long-gone Woodruff Hotel.

"You bet, we have it downstairs locked up for safe keeping," she laughed.

Region Five

CENTRAL LEATHERSTOCKING

Otsego, Broome, Chenango, Madison,
Montgomery, Oneida, Schoharie

PUSTIES

Utica

*U*tica is known as the City of Immigrants. In fact, it is because of the influx of new immigrants to this city of sixty-two thousand in the Mohawk Valley that Utica is perhaps the only Upstate New York city to *gain* in population since the last census was taken. *Reader's Digest* was one of the first national periodicals to acknowledge this when it dubbed Utica the "second chance city." New waves of Eastern Europeans and folk from the far Pacific Rim have swelled the ethnic rolls here to where now fully 20 percent of the city counts themselves as recent arrivals.

This new surge of cultures, languages, religions, and lifestyles has seemingly melded smoothly with the already established "Old World" families who settled here in the nineteenth century. Each neighborhood in Utica carries its own distinct signature. You can identify the makeup of a neighborhood by the Asian script on the small businesses, the difficult-to-pronounce names of places of worship, and the scents and aromas wafting out the front doors of bodegas, cafés, and eateries along the various side streets.

Italians were one of the largest and earliest nationalities to immigrate to the city. Their neighborhoods still thrive a century later in this heady stew of international peculiarities.

Take Bleecker Street, for example, a major east-west thoroughfare that shoots off the main business district. The Italian names along Bleecker ring with the harmonious lilt of Tuscany, Sicily, Napoli, and Roma. As I meandered down the street toward my ultimate destination, I read off the names on the old brick walls and painted on the storefront windows. I stopped in at O'scugnizzo's Pizzeria, where Eugeno Berlino, the King

Jared Alesia shows off some of the hundreds of pusties his pastry shop sells every day.

of Pizza, invented the tomato pie (a cheeseless pizza) in 1914. He sold his slices for a nickel back then. Now they are fifty cents. And well worth it. I grabbed a slice of tomato pie and continued my stroll.

I peered into the windows of Castronovo's Original Grimaldi's Restaurant, which recently shuttered after seventy years. I strolled by no fewer than a half dozen Italian bakeries, and past Garro's Drug Store, opened by Vincent deLalla in 1910. Anchoring one corner I saw Maugeri's Auto Shop, and across the street a faded window sign on a storefront read Banda Rossa Circolo Musicale. One can only imagine the ghosts enjoying themselves inside this little shop.

Of course, the neighborhood seems to nestle in the shadows of the towering twin spires of the Historic Old St. John's Roman Catholic Church at 240 Bleecker. Many generations of Italians have walked the same street to worship at this church, now almost two centuries old. When the rising morning sun catches the gold leaf-sheathed statue of St. John on the roof, beckoning the Bleecker Street faithful to come for their Sunday worship, it is an awesome sight.

And then I arrived. The Florentine Pastry Shop has been located at 667 Bleecker Street since Luigia Gennaro moved it from 605 Bleecker during World War II. The Alessandroni family took over more than a half century ago, and they are still running the shop today.

"I come from a long line of folks in this business," Jared Alesia told me. He is the newest generation to take the reins of this legendary pastry shop. He is also a trained Culinary Institute of America chef with degrees in baking and pastry arts. "I used to come in here as a kid and eat up the lemon ice and sugar cookies after school," he laughed.

After his CIA graduation, Jared heeded the generational call of the (now) Alesia family and bought the business from his parents, Debby and Andrew. His talents in the kitchen have been put to good use.

"For years, the Florentine has been known for its Old Italian standbys, and many of them are still our best sellers. I just put my own spin on those tried-and-true recipes. Like our cannolis. Our shells are all hand rolled and fried. We use impastata cheese, the highest grade ricotta cheese you can find. It is whipped and has a smooth consistency like butter. Plus you cannot buy it in grocery stores; we special order it. But it is really how we make our shells that make all the difference. I think our cannolis are the best around."

Now, let's get to the awkwardly named best seller at the Florentine.

"Ah, yes, the pusties," Jared laughed. "Actually, they are really called pasties but the pronunciation gets a little odd. Pasties are just a shortened name for the Italian dessert pasticiotti. It is a small personalized Italian pie. We make over a thousand of them a week at the pastry shop. We just can't keep them. The crust is not crunchy like a cookie, but softer like a pie. The previous generations here made them with vanilla and chocolate fillings. Once I came along I wanted to experiment so now we sell coconut pasties as well as lemon and raspberry ones. In the fall we introduced pumpkin ones and they were a big hit. They are a real Utica tradition, and you just don't find them in many places outside our area."

The pastry shop ("Don't call it a bakery, that drives my Mom crazy," Jared chuckled) seems steeped in tradition. The retail area has walls adorned with sepia-toned family pictures, maps of Italy, and photos taken by satisfied customers. One side of the shop is a café with comfortable tables and chairs. "A lot of the old timers like to come in for a coffee and a pustie and relive memories of the old days here."

The work area in the back is a nonstop beehive of activity. Jared walked me through the work stations and introduced me to his staff. A couple of workers were making dough at one table. Jared's brother Marty was busy decorating a myriad of birthday cakes at another station. Several ladies were filling what seemed to be an endless line of pusties at still another work area. We peeked around the back to where the ovens were pumping out heat as well as enticing aromas. An older Italian gentleman wearing a long white apron was shuffling huge trays of baked goods from one section of the red-hot ovens to the other. "That's Alfio Faro," Jared whispered. "My uncle taught him how to bake. He has been here for more than three decades. A real bridge to the past."

Like I said. Tradition.

With the Florentine Pastry Shop in the able hands of the newest generation, look for some surprises along with the tried and true here. Jared still oversees the making of the popular rum baba cakes. He is always testing new flavors in his pies and desserts. He is still putting Marsala wine into his tiramisu pastry cream, just like his uncles did fifty years ago. The Florentine also revolutionized the homemade gelato business by making it in small, individual squares instead of soft scooping it into a dish. This allows for two distinct flavors to be featured in each "brick." Pistachio/vanilla is a particular favorite. Lemon ices are still scooped out the old-fashioned way.

But it always comes back to tradition.

"Let me show you something, Chuck," he said as we walked back to the pastry kitchen.

"Look at these." Jared reached into one of a series of large boxes lining a side wall. He brought out a couple of small, fluted metal objects. "These are the original pustie baking tins from more than eighty years ago. We still use them every day. We believe that using the original equipment and employing a family ethic instilled in us by our forefathers, along with using only the finest ingredients available, all adds up to what makes Florentine such a special place."

Tradition.

16

HALF MOON COOKIES
Utica

*Y*ou say "black and whites," and I say "half moons."

Let's call the whole thing off. Half moon cookies it is!

They were born in Utica around 1925 at Hemstrought's Bakery. A deep, rich, cakey cookie slathered in fudge frosting on one side and white sugar frosting on the other. Of course, this unique design always leads to the great battle of "how does one eat a half moon?" Do you dive right into the chocolate side first and cleave it right up to the white sugary edge of the remaining half. Or are you a cookie rogue who likes to start right in the middle, upsetting the Gods of the Cookie World?

Harry Hemstrought introduced this iconic cookie to the world, but it was soon adapted far and wide. Almost every New York City deli features it as a dessert item, and you can even find them overseas. The Germans call the cookie the *Amerikaner* (the American).

For such a simple idea, this cookie has been embraced by pop culture through the decades. Perhaps its ultimate arrival into the upper echelons of respectability occurred when a half moon cookie was the impetus for a story arc in the popular television series *Seinfeld*.

The February 3, 1994, episode of the hit sitcom was titled "The Dinner Party." Jerry and his pals Elaine, George, and Kramer stop at a bakery to pick up a dessert to bring to a dinner party. Since they forget to take a number, they spend a good deal of time in line talking about, well, nothing. Jerry picks up a half moon cookie (called a black and white because it was filmed in New York City) and discusses his theories on race relations based on the compatibility of the black and white frosting together on the

A quartet of Hemstrought's original half moon cookies.

top of the cookie. When he tells Elaine to "look to the cookie for racial harmony," an African American customer holds up his own black and white cookie and waves back at Jerry.

With a twinkle in his eye and a nod to the *Seinfeld* show, President Obama once was given a half moon cookie while campaigning. He dubbed it the Unity Cookie.

Hemstrought's finally closed its doors several years ago, but the cookie lives on. Not that business wasn't good. They were still hand-frosting twelve thousand half moons a day at the end. But it was time to move on. The family sold its recipe to a major bakery, which sells the product today to many of the larger stores in New York, allowing customers to still grab a little bit of yesteryear when they visit a grocery store.

Jerry Hoban, a longtime employee of Hemstrought's, opened up his own popular bakery just outside of Utica. Many say the half moons at Jerry's Gingerbread Bake Shop in New Hartford are as tasty as the ones made for over seventy-five years by the original bakery.

There is no secret to the recipe of these heralded cookies. The story goes that ol' Harry Hemstrought, a former architect, wrote out the "secret" recipe and taped it up on the bakery wall years ago. I've been told it was still on the wall when the bakery closed. He was not afraid to share the recipe with any and all.

It has been shared with media outlets, cookbooks, online websites, and others. *Saveur* magazine, with a circulation of over a *third of a million readers*, posted the original Hemstrought's half moon cookie in their October 13, 2000, edition.

Their readers ate it up!

Once again the great city of Utica clocks in with another iconic Upstate food favorite. The half moon cookie . . . the best friend a cold glass of milk ever had.

Hemstrought's Original Half Moon Recipe

3¾ cups flour
¾ tsp. baking powder
2 tsp. baking soda
2¼ cups sugar
16 tbsp. cut-up butter
¾ cup sifted cocoa
¼ tsp. salt
2 eggs
1 tsp. vanilla extract
1½ cups milk

Preheat oven to 350 degrees. Sift together flour, baking powder, and baking soda in a medium bowl. Put sugar, margarine, cocoa, and salt in bowl of standing mixer and beat on medium speed until fluffy. Add eggs and vanilla and continue to beat. Add half the milk, then half the flour mixture, beating after each addition until smooth; repeat with remaining milk and flour mixture. Spoon or pipe batter onto parchment-lined baking sheets, making 3-inch rounds 2 inches apart. Bake until cookies are set, about 12 minutes. Allow to cool, then remove from parchment.

For the frostings: Use your favorite buttercream frosting for the "white" half, and your favorite fudge frosting for the "black" side.

Makes about 30 cookies.

17

CHICKEN RIGGIES

Rome

*W*hat could the old Rough Rider Teddy Roosevelt and the traditional Utica Italian dish chicken riggies possibly have in common?

Let's start with the riggies.

"We have an extensive selection of Italian American dishes on our menu, and we always like to include some surprises. But no matter how many items we prepare it is the chicken riggies that people demand. It is by far our most popular menu item," Carlos Moran told me. He is the co-owner, with Lori Bruno and Brian Miller, of one of Rome's most popular restaurants, Teddy's. "Lots of places all over the region serve riggies, but we believe ours are the best of the best. In fact, for years they used to hold a Riggie Festival in Utica to see who had the most popular chicken riggies in the area. Teddy's won it so many times they put us in the Chicken Riggie Hall of Fame," he laughed.

Make no mistake about it, this dish is served in a wide swath of Upstate New York, say from Buffalo all the way to the Capital District. But if you get out past thirty miles north or south of the New York State Thruway and ask for this item, you are more than likely to get a puzzled look from the clueless waiter. This is a dish born and raised in the Italian neighborhoods of the Utica-Rome area.

In fact the whole area is worthy of its own "Taste of . . ." book. Turkey Joints candy, pusties, half moon cookies, and chicken riggies are the anointed ones in this book. But that is only because I needed to share the spotlight with other Upstate cities. I could have added tomato pie, Utica greens, and baked hats to the list, but that would be a classic food

Carlos and Michelle Moran show off their signature dish, chicken riggies. It's the best, and they have the awards to prove it!

"pile-on." Maybe they can be featured in a future book because each one of them is worthy of individual praise in this region known for its unique and tasty food traditions.

"Yes, everybody makes riggies," Michelle Moran, Carlos's wife said. "However, we make ours a little different. When Carlos first bought this restaurant we decided to change some items and leave other things as they were. The riggies have always been a staple of the Utica-Rome area, but Carlos put his unique spin on the dish."

"Some places make riggies with penne pasta," Carlos interjected. "That is just not right. You must use rigatoni pasta for the riggies, which is how they got their name. We use boneless chicken breasts, never frozen. We add white wine to our homemade Alfredo sauce and sauté our peppers, onions, and mushrooms. We add a few of our own secret spices to it and, well, it works. We sell over a hundred bowls of chicken riggies each and every day. Our customers keep coming back week after week, month after month ordering our riggies. And we do a lot of catering, too. And with every catering order, *every one*, the food list must include our home-made chicken riggies.

"Ask anyone on the street who makes the best Italian food anywhere and they will usually tell you their mothers or grandmothers. Well, we like to think that Teddy's is right up there next to Grandma's," he smiled.

Co-owner Brian Miller stopped by our table during my visit to Teddy's. I asked him what sets his restaurant apart from so many of the others in the area.

"Speaking for myself, it is the people. The staff and the customers. They are all wonderful. I can hardly make it from the front door to the back without having to stop at each table for a chat and a hello. No two days are alike at Teddy's, and it is still fun to work at a place that means so much to so many people. They have been coming in here for our riggies for a very long time, and I know they will be coming in for yet an even longer time. It is a warm place, a place connected to the community. Like a trusty old friend, but one who makes exceptional food. In fact, frankly, after my wife, this place is my family."

Both Mr. and Mrs. Moran come from food service backgrounds. "Carlos was born in Mexico and ended up in San Diego. I met him when we were both working at the El Torito restaurant. I was the cocktail server, and he had risen to executive chef. We married and eventually had three small children. Out of the blue Carlos got an offer to come to Upstate New York to be the chef at the Alexander Hamilton Hotel in Clinton."

I asked if the transition from West Coast to Upstate was seamless.

"I didn't know anybody or anything about Upstate," Carlos said with a loud laugh. "Nothing. I thought all of New York was New York City. People in San Diego said 'Are you crazy? Out of your mind?' So before I accepted the job, I came here all by myself to spend a week in Upstate checking it out. Needless to say, I fell in love with the area and the people, and I knew that I, that *we*, had found our new home.

"After a short stint at the Alexander Hamilton Hotel, this place became available. It was a long-established restaurant, and we bought it with Lori and Brian. At the time, it was kind of a plastic tablecloth place serving diner food like sandwiches and burgers. I had loftier ideas, and what you see now is my dream come true."

Teddy's is tucked away in a strip mall just outside of the Rome downtown area. There are two parts to Teddy's. One side features comfortable booths and tables and a cozy pub in the back. The other side is an attractive larger room for banquets, catered affairs, and more dining. And there isn't a plastic tablecloth to be found.

"They went first," Michelle smiled. "And we brought in a large selection of Tiffany lighting to give the place a warm, yet sophisticated, aura. But we did keep all the Teddys," she said.

The restaurant is wall-to-wall Teddy Roosevelt. Family photos, paintings, historical artifacts, documents and campaign memorabilia. Some are reproductions and some are valuable archival items. And the shelves along the top of the restaurant walls are populated with teddy bears. Big ones, small ones, collectible ones, new ones and old ones.

So what is it about Teddy Roosevelt here?

"The previous owner was a big fan and collector of Teddy Roosevelt memorabilia, and he displayed it all over the restaurant. After some thought, we adopted Teddy because of what he stood for. We are near the Adirondacks, and he was a key early American conservationist who sought to protect the wilds. He came through the area several times when he was governor of New York, and both Carlos and I like his philosophy on life. His passion, courage, sensitivity, and 'speak softly but carry a big stick' really tells the story of our lives."

So how does a place whose interior combines fluffy teddy bears with Tiffany lamps pull it all off? Quite well, actually.

Especially when you are staring down one of the most delectable Italian food dishes in all of Central New York. Teddy Roosevelt may have been president of the United States, but chicken riggies rule the day at this memorable landmark restaurant.

18

TURKEY JOINTS CANDY

Rome

*D*on't blink or you will miss Nora's Candy Shop at 321 North Doxtator Street in Rome.

"Yes, even though we have been here for almost a century, we do like to keep a low profile," Spero Haritatos told me. The deceivingly small store front masks a ten-thousand-square-foot operation that has been churning out Turkey Joints candy since 1919. And all from the same location.

"The whole thing started with my immigrant relatives. My dad and his nine brothers. They came over from Greece in 1919 and opened up this candy shop," Spero told me as he waved his hand around a space filled with counters, showcases, and work areas. "We lived on one side of the building and worked on the other. Nora's is now known for the Turkey Joints but we also make custom chocolate molds into almost anything imaginable, from animals, to people, to cars and even dinosaurs. Over the years it ended up my parents' business," he said as he pointed to the sepia toned photographs of his parents, Nora and Tasos, on the showroom wall overseeing the operation. "And then I came along," he chuckled.

Like so many other entries in this book, perhaps the overriding theme is that of a real familial attachment to the business. So many owners have told me how they were literally brought up in the factory or store or restaurant that they now own.

Nora's is no different.

"I grew up right here in these rooms," Spero said. "It is a close-knit residential neighborhood, and we just blended in and became a part of it. We were the only business on a block filled with houses. Everybody

Owner Sharon Mazur-Haritatos proudly displays her family's iconic candy. They ship Turkey Joints nationwide.

knew everybody. Even our school, Gansevoort Elementary School, is only a couple of doors down. I went there and then worked in the candy shop after school ever since I was a boy. During the peak of candy making season the teachers at the school knew that they would have one empty seat in their classroom. Every Christmas my parents made an arrangement with the school for me to be absent for two weeks to work in the shop with them making the Turkey Joints," he laughed. "I used to play football, but Dad made me come to work on Saturdays. I have been here steadily since I was twelve years old. I sure missed a lot of dances because of this old candy store," he smiled.

So what is a Turkey Joint candy anyway? Sharon, Spero's wife, took over the conversation here.

"It's an old candy. We really do not know where the idea came from. But all the elder Greek immigrants in the family evidently brought the concept and recipe over here from the old country, and we have been making them on North Doxtator Street since 1919."

Spero and Sharon took me on a tour of the production area.

"Turkey Joints are a seemingly simple candy as far as ingredients go. Just some spun sugar coating, which covers a filling of chocolate and Brazil nuts. But it is the unique shape that people love. They are hand rolled into an odd formation that really does look like a turkey leg, joint and all," said Sharon.

Visiting the work area is like taking a trip back to the founding days of the candy shop. All that is lacking is the sound of the patois of the Greek Islands as the original Haritatos boys spun their sugary wonders. The equipment is old, most of it original to 1919, and surprisingly functional.

"The stove is from the opening of the shop," Spero continued as we moved through the candy making area. "We use only these old large copper kettles to boil our confections in. The long candy work tables are topped with thick white marble slabs. The long homemade spinning table is also original, and this is where the candy takes on its unique shape. Every step of the process is done by hand. We have cutting machines that are original to the opening of the shop and we also have this monster right here."

Spero was standing under a demonic metal hook that spears out of the back wall looking to snare an unsuspecting customer. "Yes, the kids are always surprised to see this thing," he laughed. "This hook is where we drape our confections to aerate them before they are cut." It was sinister looking, I must admit.

In the back are the standard loading dock and storage areas. At the end of our tour, Spero opened a heavy door and we walked into a large cooler. This room held cases and cases of packaged Turkey Joints ready to be shipped out. "Each jar holds twelve ounces of candy, a dozen Turkey Joints per jar."

There must have been thousands of them in the cooler ready to go.

The making of this unique candy is seasonal.

"We do not ship our candy from May to October. We just can't do it because the heat will distort the unusual shiny gloss that our spun sugar gives each joint. So we stack them up and get ready for candy season."

"When exactly is candy season?" I asked.

"Christmas!" was the emphatic answer from this husband and wife team. "Ninety percent of our business is wholesale. Major supermarkets like Wegmans, Price Chopper, Hannaford, and others take our Turkey Joints all over the state. We still have a few local customers who come in to buy them. Not many. Mostly the old timers who love to come here for sentimental reasons. But at Christmas it gets real crazy in here."

"We are only a small group working here," Sharon said. "Myself, Spero, my sister Karen and her daughter, Breanna. That's pretty much it. And the orders that come in for thousands of Turkey Joints really keep us jumping during the holiday season. We even enlist the help of our best friend, Marlene, to come join in. She's been doing it every year for more than twenty years. That's what friends are for!

"People call in, mail in, order online or just stop in. It is just wild. On our busiest days before Christmas we can ship as many as fifteen hundred cases of joints on a single day through Fed Ex or UPS."

I had never had a Turkey Joint before I stopped in at the unassuming white building on North Doxtator to meet this lovely couple. They corrected that immediately. They plied me with the candy during my visit, and I was hooked. Each joint is a significant piece of delicious sweetness, with just the right crunch on the outside and a delectable nutty kind of chocolate reward inside. Millions of these quirky treats have left through the doors of Nora's since 1919. And yes, they do look just like a turkey joint.

It looks like this candy won't disappear any time soon.

"My Mom died in 1982, and I took over the business the very next day," Spero said. "My dad died in 1993, and Sharon took over for him. One of the first things we did was trademark the name and design of the Turkey Joints. My family has put too much love and hard work into the product for me to ever let it go away."

It is wonderful that this young couple continues to honor the memory of a long line that came before them by keeping this cherished business going strong into the twenty-first century.

I think an old Greek proverb says it best concerning Spero and Sharon: "Honor is priceless and glad are they who have it."

19

SPIEDIES

Binghamton

*W*hen you start rooting around to find the origins of this signature Broome County delicacy, you come face to face with Old World traditions, straightforward recipes from the old country, and classic early-twentieth-century Southern Tier names like Iacovelli, Sharak, Salamida, and Lupo. The sandwich's name came from the Italian word spiedini, which refers to any cubed meat cooked over a charcoal grill and served on skewers.

Most historians give credit to the brothers Camillo and Augie Iacovelli as the creators of spiedies. They were serving them in their family restaurants and bars well back into the 1930s. Today spiedies are served throughout the Southern Tier at every imaginable venue, from ballparks to concert halls to street festivals to house parties. Ask a dozen people where the best spiedie is in the Triple Cities and you will get a dozen answers. The Spiedie and Rib Pit on Front Street. The Char Pit in Endicott. Sharkey's over on Glenwood Avenue, where, perhaps, the first cubes of lamb were grilled and slid off their skewers onto a fresh slice of Italian bread. The list is endless.

But over on West State Street, just north of downtown Binghamton, now there is a place! A place that is steeped in Italian history, was the original creator of the chicken spiedie, sells over one thousand pounds of marinated spiedie meat a week, has been featured on the Food Network and in the *New York Times*, and has been host to three generations of food lovers since it first opened its doors.

And it is all in what once was a Dairy Queen!

The home of Binghamton's signature sandwich: the spiedie. The sandwich even has a festival named after it.

"My father, Sam Lupo, had a small corner grocery store in Endicott he owned with his brother John," Stephen Lupo told me. "It was at 1407 Watson Boulevard and was a typical mom and pop store, but they specialized in custom cut meats, so that separated us from the other dozens of markets that were around back then. We found that a lot of people would do their grocery shopping at the big markets and then come to our store to get their meat. My dad sold spiedie meat back then, but he never cooked it. Big chunks of prime pork and lamb marinated in his own special sauce."

Sam Lupo Jr., Stephen's brother, picked up the family story from here.

"It was a great little grocery store, and I got my start in the business working there as a kid. Our dad and uncle had a large and loyal customer base. I remember that they even had a little tin box under the cash register for their credit customers. They would keep track of the purchases on three-by-five cards. We had a lot of big businesses around us back then like Endicott-Johnson Shoes, IBM, Singer Link and others. On pay day, they would all come in and pay their account at the market. It was that kind of a place."

"Eventually, like so many things do, the spiedie business caught on and my father and Uncle John opened up this restaurant. It was my decision to close down the little market and move the family business in a new direction," Sam told me. "Closing down your family business is a pretty serious decision, but I knew we had to move forward. The economy was in a downturn, and the big supermarkets were just killing us. So we did it. And this restaurant is really where our spiedies began."

The restaurant, opened in 1978, is Lupo's S&S Char Pit. If there is a mecca for spiedie lovers, this is it.

"This used to be a Dairy Queen, but we have expanded it over the years. We started grilling our famous marinated pork, and our customers, both old and new, really responded well to it. We became well known all around Binghamton. A funny thing happened shortly after we opened. Originally we sold lamb spiedies, but lamb prices were going through the roof, so we stuck with pork only. Then my dad got ill with heart problems. I decided one day to start grilling up chicken spiedies, something that was unheard of at the time. I figured that skinless, boneless chicken breasts cooked in corn oil would be a healthy substitute for our more traditional spiedies, so I put the chicken spiedie on the menu really as a way to get my dad and everybody else to eat healthier."

A chicken spiedie was about as dramatic a change as one could make to this classic lamb and pork sandwich that was a favorite of the shepherds working their flocks in the mountains of Italy in the late 1800s.

Stephen reached over and patted his older brother on the shoulder. "My brother, the inventor of the chicken spiedie," he said with a grin.

So how did it go?

"It was an unmitigated disaster," Sam said as both brothers broke out in a loud laugh. "Total flop. Nobody wanted the new sandwich. 'A chicken spiedie? Are you crazy?' they said to me. I couldn't give them away. I knew I was in big trouble."

So what happened?

"I honestly have no idea. We kept at it, kept pushing the new sandwich, kept suggesting it to our customers and slowly, very slowly, the chicken spiedie began to take off. Many of the college students who came here started to choose it over the lamb or pork. Soon, miracle of miracles, the chicken spiedie became, and still is, far and away our top seller."

So how did it feel, finally, to be the Spiedie King at such a young age?

"Well, I came home from college one weekend and my father sat me down for a talk. My Uncle John had died unexpectedly leaving my dad alone in the business. And his own health was failing. Dad asked me to give 'give him one year' so he could figure out what he was going to do. I agreed. That was 1978 and I am still here. Some year, huh?" he smiled.

Spiedies have taken on a mythical reputation in the Triple Cities. They are the iconic sandwich of this region, found almost nowhere else outside of, say, a one hundred mile area. People come into Lupo's and order them by the bagful. There is almost no time when there is not a small mountain of chicken or pork cubes sizzling away on the huge grills.

And the brothers have branched out into two separate arenas. Stephen manages the restaurant, and brother Sam oversees the large USDA meat facility in Endicott from which Lupo's meat products are shipped out to most of the major supermarkets in Upstate New York and northern Pennsylvania.

"We continue to grow and to expand, always looking over the horizon but never letting go of our past. We owe absolutely everything to the hard work and dedication of my father and my uncle who began all of this over a half century ago. Our mother, Carol, is now ninety years old and still with us. My brother and I are the caretakers of the spiedie legend. And it isn't stopping there either. My own son, Eliott, is the assistant manager of the restaurant and is our outdoor events coordinator. The circle keeps growing, and that is a good thing," Sam said.

"So the spiedie story has survived despite that 'total disaster' back when you first introduced the chicken spiedie?" I asked Sam.

"Yes, and that wasn't the only hurdle we had to overcome. We used to send our spiedie meat to our friends and family. Nothing standardized, just on a casual basis. Well, one day a writer for the *New York Times* came in for lunch. We got chatting, and he said he wanted to write about this new wonder of a sandwich called a spiedie. The next week the *Times* published his article, and in it he misquoted us by saying that you could order

Lupo's spiedies by mail. The next day our phone started ringing off the wall. I was totally misquoted but the callers wanted none of that. They wanted spiedies! We didn't even have a credit card machine," Stephen laughed.

"I had no idea how to even ship perishable items, so I ordered up some Omaha Steaks by phone, and when they arrived I studied them to see how they were packaged, how they were shipped with dry ice, everything. So, one little sentence in the *New York Times* and there we were—a mail order business."

Today you can buy Lupo's products online, by mail, by phone or at the annual Spiedie Fest and Balloon Rally held every summer.

"Spiedie Fest has gone through the roof. Everybody comes to it from all over the Northeast. It is one of the key fundraisers for many area non-profits. We like being a part of it. Anything we can do for our community to give back is good with us. Plus it is crazy out there. They have big concerts, spiedie cook-offs, all kinds of things. It is the biggest event in our city. We sell ten thousand spiedie sandwiches over a single weekend at Spiedie Fest," Stephen told me.

Sam Lupo Sr. once sat his two sons down and told them something both of them remember to this day. He told them, "If it is necessary to raise your prices five cents, then do it. But never ever cut back on quality."

"Our Old World upbringing, quality product, and our legion of customers speak for themselves, and it all goes back to that little mom and pop corner grocery store at 1407 Watson Boulevard in Endicott with my dad and my Uncle John," Sam said as I was leaving.

I wondered. Is that little grocery store still there?

"Yes," he winked. "It's a Chinese restaurant now."

20

MOLASSES CRINKLES

Fly Creek

To call a molasses crinkle just a cookie is to do a serious injustice to the art of baking. Eating one of these impossible-to-put-down treats is akin to a trip down memory lane, like receiving a hug from your dear old grandmother.

"My own grandmother, Jane Michaels, started baking these cookies in her very own kitchen oven at 202 Main Street in Cooperstown back in the late 1930s," Bill Michaels told me. Bill and his wife, Brenda, are the owners of the Fly Creek Cider Mill.

"I remember that I would usually eat real food down at my parents' grocery store, things like meat and vegetables. And then I would head on over to my grandmother's house for dessert. You'd walk into her home and the aroma of the molasses cookies would just knock you over. It's a wonderful memory."

Eventually Grandma's cookies made it over to the gift and snack area of the Fly Creek Cider Mill. "Yes, Brenda and I have owned the mill since 1999. I was brought up here as a kid, and the mill itself is well over 150 years old."

The Fly Creek Cider Mill is a shining example of a small family business that has grown and expanded over the years, all the while nurturing a beloved tradition in Central New York.

"As our business has grown, so has the number of our visitors," Brenda Michaels told me. "We now see second and even third generations coming here, mothers with kids and grandparents with little ones in the strollers. They come for the cider, they come to feed the ducks in our pond,

The Fly Creek Cider Mill's famous molasses crinkle cookie—still made with Grandma Michaels's 1930 recipe.

and they come to relive their own warm memories of visiting us when they were younger. I really believe that one of our missions at the mill is to set some traditions for families in the future. It is a fun place."

The Fly Creek Cider Mill now includes a wide variety of foods for their customers to buy. "Of course we are famous for our samplings," Bill said. "On any given day you can come into our store and sample more than forty different food products, from our famous cheeses to our fudge, homemade salsas, ciders, and snack items. People love to sample their way around the marketplace while loading up their shopping baskets," he laughed.

The mill sits along the bubbling Fly Creek surrounded by Norman Rockwell–inspired apple orchards and gently rolling hills. The hamlet of the same name is just a speck on the map, a deep-fly-ball's distance from the National Baseball Hall of Fame, which is just over the hill.

"Our cider mill is one of the most historic mills you will find in the state. Hosea Williams started it all 150-plus years ago when he built a centralized cider mill along the creek to press cider from his apples. We still use the original 1889 Boomer and Boschert apple press he bought in Syracuse. And it is rare in that it is still water powered and water hydraulic. We press more than twenty thousand gallons of apple cider a year out of that trusty piece of equipment," Bill said.

A recent venture at the mill is the making of an apple cider wine. During the cold months, they freeze and refreeze their McIntosh, Empire, Cortland, and Macoun apple ciders to make Apple Frost wine. The mill is now a stop on the popular Cooperstown Beverage Trail.

As the mill business morphed from a rural cider-pressing business to more of a tourist destination, the amenities offered here have multiplied as well.

"We have an extensive gift shop, and our marketplace continues to grow every year. We have a food stand, so our visitors can stay and have lunch with us, and we even have a very active online business," Brenda Michaels said. "It does get busy around the mill. I started working here for a year before Bill was even here, just to see if it was something I would like. Actually, I thought I would because I'd only have to work one hundred days a year," she smiled. "I don't know whatever happened to that! But it is a wonderful place to work and I really enjoy every minute of it. Of course, the customers are what make it so special for me. It is amazing. We watch teenagers come in with their parents. Like other young people, they are usually buried in their cell phones texting away when they get here. Pretty soon the phones disappear and you can see them laughing out by the pond feeding the ducks. It really is a magical place."

So how did the molasses crinkles get their name?

"Well, my grandmother really knew how to bake," Bill began. "She used only the best ingredients. For these cookies she used Horn of Plenty molasses, which comes from the Caribbean island of Barbados. It is a product of the first boiling off of the sugar cane so it has a much lighter, cleaner taste than most brands of molasses. I think that is really the secret to their popularity. Our cookie dough is made by our friends in Oneida at the Madison/Cortland ARC. They employ folks with intellectual and other developmental disabilities. They are great. They make the dough using my grandmother's very own 1930s recipe. We then do all the baking ourselves at the mill. We have two huge Garland ovens and we make them

288 cookies at a time. And we bake them all day long, every day during the height of the season."

So now, after selling about thirty thousand cookies a season for decades, what is the magic that makes these cookies so special?

"People just love them. They tell us they are old-fashioned tasting, like they had when they were kids. The cookies are soft, moist and chewy unlike a ginger snap. There is a distinct molasses flavor to them, and we top them off with large sugar sprinkles. They are in the oven for just twelve minutes, and when the tops start cracking and get all crinkled up we know they are done. That is how they got the name molasses crinkles."

Because baseball is the centerpiece of this region, the tourist season can be pretty hectic at the mill. "We get more than 150,000 visitors a year," Brenda told me. "A lot of them are baseball families, and they take their memories of the mill back home with them. We see that in our ever-growing mail order business. We ship from New York to California and everywhere in between."

It is all about the family experience at the Fly Creek Cider Mill. There are games for kids to play, there is a viewing area where you can see the old press grind and squeeze bushels of apples at a time, and there are cartoon characters on the buildings and fences to amuse the little ones. And there are the ducks.

"Yes, those ducks and geese out there are the stars of the show," Lindora Molloy said. She is the mill's lead manager and has been here since the beginning.

"I have seen it all. This is my passion. I do all the buying and employee interaction. We have a great staff, many of whom have been here for more than a decade. I do a lot of the online processing, and you just never know who is going to be on the other end of the phone or the emails. It is just a fun, lively place where the family comes first."

At the mention of the phrase "family experience" Brenda gave out with a laugh. "Yes, the family comes first for sure. In fact I was pregnant with our first child when we had our Grand Opening Day. That morning I felt like I was coming down with the flu or a cold so I drove over to Cooperstown to the hospital just to check it out. Much to my surprise, my doctor told me I didn't have the flu, I was in labor! I called Bill back here at the mill to tell him to get over here. Of course, he was up to his neck with customers on our very first day in business. He grabbed a disposable camera from the gift shop and raced over here. He made it just in time. I was admitted at noon and delivered our daughter, Sadie Joyce Michaels, at 1:30. And there was my husband snapping away with his disposable camera still wearing his Fly Creek Cider Mill uniform," she laughed.

As I said goodbye to this lovely couple I just had to ask.

"After a million molasses crinkles have been made and gobbled up since the 1930s, and with their fame spreading so far and wide, did this legendary cookie's fame really begin in that little kitchen at 202 Main Street in Cooperstown?"

"It sure did. My grandmother was the classic spoiler grandmother and *everybody* got one of her famous cookies," Bill said.

Region Six

ADIRONDACKS/NORTH COUNTRY

Franklin, Clinton, Essex, Herkimer, Hamilton, Warren, Fulton, Lewis

21

CROGHAN BOLOGNA
Croghan

$\mathcal{D}$o you remember the old *What's My Line?* television show? The premise of the show is that an ordinary person would come out and whisper their unordinary accomplishment or profession to the host, John Charles Daley. For example a short man would be a skyscraper construction worker, or a little old lady would be a sheriff. Well if there was a time tunnel back to that show in the 1950s, you could certainly put Blaine Campany in the guest chair. Nobody would ever guess the profession of this attractive new college graduate.

She is a butcher. And she owns the legendary Croghan Meat Market.

Known for its homemade bologna, this tiny little market just outside the Blue Line of the Adirondack Park has a reputation that literally goes around the country. "Yes, we sell a lot of bologna rings through the mail," Blaine told me. "Folks from around here who grew up and moved away love it as a nostalgic souvenir of their youth. Of course this region is loaded with tourists throughout the summer. They come from all over the country and a lot of them stop in here. So that is how the word has spread about our meats."

Even though she is a fresh-faced 2012 graduate of the State University of New York at Brockport, Blaine has been around the business since she was a child. "I learned all of my butchering from my dad. My family goes back four generations at this market. Usually all the women, including my mother, my aunts, grandmothers, and others worked in the back. All the men did the butchering. That is, until I came along," she said with a laugh.

Blaine Campany is the newest generation of her family to operate one of the North Country's legendary meat markets.

The market is very small. Just inside the front door you will find a meat case loaded with fresh cut loins, shoulder butts, chops, T-bones, and prime ribs. But more often than not, when the front door signals its "ding-a-ling" it means someone is coming in for their famous Croghan bologna.

"The original recipe came over with the founders of the market in 1888. It has been handed down through the decades ever since. We make it by touch and feel. The mixing and the stuffing of the rings take about six hours. The whole process takes about two days from start to finish. We are very finicky about our bologna. I can feel and sense when it is done. And when we put it out for sale, well, it doesn't last very long in the case," she told me.

So what is so special about Croghan bologna?

"It's funny you asked that. A lot of people have asked me to give them the recipe. I always tell them that I could give it to them but it wouldn't make any difference. I tell them it is not just a ring of bologna. It is the sentimentality of the good old days. Of the people who make it now and have made it for well over a century. All right here in this little building. It is the love and care we put into our product. That is what they are buying. And that is what the people want."

The market ships bologna cold by UPS to anywhere in the country. Blaine's father, John, is mostly retired now but still enjoys doing the deliveries. "He is a chatterbox and loves to visit with the customers," she smiled. They sell and deliver to stores in a one hundred mile radius.

Blaine has a head for business and a knack with a butcher knife. She is now on the Board of Directors of the Lowville Chamber of Commerce and oversees all facets of the business, from the smokehouse to the ledger books to the marketing to the chopping block.

"I love working in this business. It means so much to me to be the newest in a long line of family members serving the local people. It does get pretty busy, especially in the summer with all the campers coming by. The Fourth of July is crazy in here, too. During the Christmas holidays we can ship a few hundred boxes of bologna in a single day. People really enjoy giving our bologna rings as a holiday gift. It seems everybody wants the biggest ring of bologna we can make for their boss or family member or special friend. We have made them as big as six pounds, and believe me that is a lot of bologna," she told me.

As I was waiting at the counter for Blaine to wrap up my own special ring of Croghan's bologna, I asked her if she ever gets a funny look from some of the customers who may not know that she is a meat cutter. "Oh, yes," she said with a big grin. "Mostly women. I've had them come in while I've been behind the counter. I ask them if I can help them and they say, 'Yes, dear, is the butcher in so *he* can cut my meat for me?' They are shocked when I tell them that I am the butcher."

And what about the male customers?

"The men are fascinated by it. They'll say, 'Did you really just cut that?' It is funny."

The Croghan Meat Market is a storied place in a land of beauty. Kind of like the general store up on Walton's Mountain. The business has been in the same family's hands since the 1800s and there is no doubt that Blaine Campany is the right person, the right butcher, the right woman to take them well into the future.

22

PHILADELPHIA CREAM CHEESE
Lowville

*T*hose little foil bricks of Philadelphia cream cheese started their trek northward through New York State in 1872 beginning in Chester (Orange County). From there we follow the story to Edmeston (Otsego County) and finally we end our journey in Lowville (Lewis County). Notice the cream cheese trail never once went through Philadelphia?

Let me explain.

William A. Lawrence, a dairyman from Chester, came up with the process of making a smooth, spreadable cheese product to utilize all the dairy elements being produced in his home area. A lot of milk was coming out of the rich pasturelands of Orange County, but New York City, a tantalizing and lucrative market just down the Hudson River, was still too far away in the day and age of no refrigeration. So cream cheese took its place as a major cash crop. Unlike the typical hard cheese of its day, cream cheese had a higher fat content and was spreadable. Lawrence patented his product and sought a sophisticated name for his new spread.

In the later 1800s, the City of Brotherly Love was considered to be one of the most dynamic cities in the country. A center for commerce, culture, and academia. For this, and no other reason, Lawrence named his product Philadelphia Cream Cheese, and the great deception began.

In 1885, a company surrogate, the Empire Cheese factory in rural Edmeston patented the name "Philadelphia" for the product. That factory burned down and was rebuilt and christened the Phenix Cheese Company in tribute to its resiliency. Phenix was bought by food giant Kraft Foods in 1928.

Lowville's unofficial dairy mascot is this giant cow statue. Her name is LeWinda Milkzalot. She has become one of the most popular photo ops in the Land of Cream Cheese.

Cream cheese had a very limited shelf life once it was opened. The company invented the little signature foil wrappers to lengthen the life of the product. Foil keeps light and heat at bay and prevents oxidation.

So we have now followed the "silver brick road" from Chester up to Edmeston. But it is in the ninety-mile jump to northern Lowville that things really start to get fun.

The Kraft factory in Lowville is the largest cream cheese manufacturing plant in the world. This major North Country employer creates Philadelphia Cream Cheese as the final product of an amalgamation of more than two hundred local dairy farmers who belong to the Kraft Co-op (founded in the Great Depression). A retail outlet remains busy all day long with locals coming in to buy all kinds of regional foods, including the famous cream cheese. The huge factory is right next door to the store.

Lowville shouts its cream cheese pride at the top of its lungs. First of all, there is Lady LaWinDa Milkzalot. This fiberglass cow is the largest bovine idol in America. She stands almost ten feet tall and is fifteen feet long. Usually adorned with a funny hat or an oversized pair of sunglasses, Lady, located near the factory, is one of the most popular photo opportunities in the area.

The employees of the Kraft factory here take their cream cheese seriously, but not too seriously. Every year, Lowville hosts an annual Cream Cheese Festival that swells the village to triple in size. They culminate the festivities with the baking of the world's largest cheesecake (some seven thousand pounds and counting).

Philadelphia Cream Cheese got its passport punched in 1960. It was off to Merry Olde England.

Lowville's cream cheese stormed the shores of Great Britain in the 1960s and has become something of a sensation ever since. Philadelphia UK even has its own Facebook page with over two hundred thousand friends catching up on new flavors and the latest recipes, and just sharing their own memories of their favorite spread. Cream cheese in the UK tastes a little different than our favorite here in the states. In Britain, cream cheese must have a minimum 45 to 65 percent fat content for a super-rich, creamy taste. The allowed minimum fat content in the United States is 33 percent for all brands including Philadelphia.

In England, where the cream cheese is the top seller, a website once asked for recipes from its readers that used Philadelphia as a key ingredient. At last look more than five hundred recipes (and counting) were included in the survey. Today Kraft makes more than three dozen different cream cheese flavors, including garden vegetable, pumpkin spice, Italian cheese and herb, cracked pepper, and salmon. The original, plain flavor is still their best seller.

While Lowville celebrates its cream cheese pedigree with fun, festivals, and a fifteen-foot-long plastic cow, you will be hard pressed to find any outward boast in Chester. The first stop on the cream cheese trail, though, is definitely worth a look.

Chester is a historic community with roots reaching back to the dawning of America. Be sure and take a look at the Yelverton Inn. It is one of those places you see throughout the Hudson Valley with signs out front reading "George Washington Slept Here." Only it is true.

General Washington crawled into the sack here on the night of July 27, 1782.

If you visit Chester, a village of about four thousand residents, you might enjoy a bagel and a schmear at any of the several coffee shops downtown. And when you do, you will no doubt understand that there is just something historically romantic about slathering on some pearly white Philadelphia cream cheese in the place of its birth.

23

POUTINE

Malone

*I*f you live south of the Tug Hill Plateau, chances are you have no idea how to pronounce the name of this chapter's subject—and therein lies one of two opportunities to start a lively debate among aficionados of this Quebecois treat!

All French-Canadian traditionalists, repeat after me: "Poo-tin".

Everyone else, repeat after me: "Poo-teen"

One can also successfully stir passions over the matter of cheese, but more about that later.

Poutine has been slowly migrating down from the Canadian border for three decades or more. Although well established in its native country (some Canadian McDonald's have poutine on their menus), the dish is as rare as finding a fresh Hudson Valley ramp below the foothills of the Catskills.

Never heard of a Hudson ramp? Oh well, let's move on.

On its face, poutine is one of the simplest dishes in this book. Many of us have been eating it for a half century or more and we don't even know it. I first had my own poutine-like experience when I was eighteen years old. After long nights of carousing the bars with my college friends we would usually end up at a diner or truck stop to top off the night with some good solid comfort food. That food was usually French fries with brown gravy. Lots of gravy. Sometimes, when asked if we wanted "cheese fries," we'd basically end up with a poor man's version of poutine.

But there are so many nuances to the dish that were missing in those all night diners and dives of my youth. First the fries must be cooked

Dene Savage, Marketing and IT Director, joins Angel Warner, Food and Beverage Manager, for some poutine after a busy day at the ski center.

to a crispiness that will endure their swim in the gravy. The gravy must always be brown (although Quebecois will add in their own secret spices and flavors), and the cheese should be curdy, although this component is evolving. Still, with just fries, gravy, and cheese, well, it is pretty hard to mess this dish up.

The North Country is proliferate with poutine palaces. Many of them are seasonal (like a lot of North Country places) and are shuttered between Labor Day and Memorial Day. Poutine has made it onto the menu of several quality eateries from Lake Champlain to Clayton to Oswego. Yes, the St. Lawrence Seaway is poutine country.

Many area locals go to Olive Ridley's in Plattsburgh for their poutine fix. This place is comfort food heaven, serving everything from ribs to nachos to crab cakes. Open all year, Olive Ridley's serves some of the best poutine you'll find under the border. Plattsburgh is just an hour south of Montreal, where poutineries can be found on every corner. Ridley's will also mix in some pulled pork if you wish, making a unique variation on the original.

Word of this French Canadian favorite has reached the far corners of New York (and Vermont, New Hampshire, and Maine), and even some top notch restaurants in Manhattan are now serving it. You can also find it in the oddest places, like New York State Thruway rest stops, street vendors, and even at the famous Dinosaur Bar-B-Que in Syracuse. They have it on their classic meat and potatoes menu (although they feature pimento cheese instead of cheese curds in their poutine).

One of the oddest places I have ever sampled poutine was from a food truck. It was at LarkFest in Albany, Upstate's largest street festival. I caught a glimpse of a fancily painted food truck in the dining section of the festival. There was no line, and what they were serving looked oddly familiar. It was the poutine food truck! I ordered up a large portion, and it was delicious. Substantial sized French fries (cut and fried while you wait) slathered with a deep rich brown gravy and then covered with slowly melting, squeaking cheese curds sprinkled over the top like little yellow pillows. It was hot, tasty, and among the best examples of poutine I've ever had. By all accounts, Le Petit Poutine food truck out of Rochester is by far the best of the mobile poutine providers popping up all over Upstate.

Some may quest for silver or gold or riches untold, but if your quest should be for the perfect poutine, may I suggest heading to a small family-run ski resort deep in the North Country almost within sight of the Canadian border.

At Titus Mountain Family Ski Center you will find, in my opinion, *poutine c'est magnifique!*

"Yes, we do make a great poutine," Dene Savage told me. He is the Director of Marketing and Information Technology at Titus Mountain located just seven miles south of Malone.

Titus Mountain is a mid-sized ski area featuring three mountains, two lodges, ten lifts, forty-four trails, a tubing park, and even an offer of night skiing. There are also several dining facilities at Titus.

"Approximately half of our patronage comes across the border from Canada. That total can reach twenty-five thousand some years. And with all of these French Canadians skiing at Titus, you know we have to have an excellent poutine on our menu. We serve it both at our upscale dining facility, Mo's Moon Valley Grill, as well as at our more casual cafeterias. It is a very popular item."

How popular, I asked?

"Well, at the busy times, like around holidays when we are packed with skiers, we can expect to prepare as many as two hundred plates of poutine or more on a single day."

Dene clearly has eaten his share of poutine. He waxes eloquent about the dish, its presentation, and the different nuances about poutine served at various other places. His knowledge of poutine is, if it is possible, encyclopedic.

"Yes, I've enjoyed poutine for a very long time," he laughed. "It really is an excellent dish and we take great care to make the best possible poutine we can. It starts with our French fries. They are, of course, the foundation upon which the rest of the house is built. We use a lightly battered fry that comes to us with the skins still on. They are a medium cut, about halfway between a string fry and a wedge. Just enough to satisfactorily hold the gravy and the cheese.

"The next step is to deep fry our poutine potatoes just a little bit longer than we would fry a regular order of fries. We believe that the whole ingredient to our poutine being superior is how we deep fry our potatoes. We cook them in soy bean oil and leave them in the fryer just a little bit longer than normal. This gives them a rich golden color and makes them crispy and sturdy. Nobody wants a limp fry after all.

"The fryers we use are unique in that they are self-cleaning the oil all the time. As the fries are cooking the oil is constantly being cleaned. This cuts down on the amount of smoke emitted by the fryers as well as allowing us to cook the fries at a higher temperature. Our poutine fries are much less resistant to going limp when the gravy is poured over them because of this method of cooking. It really does make all the difference in the taste and texture," he told me.

"For our gravy we always use a brown, beef gravy that is lightly seasoned and cooked to a perfect consistency so it will move down through the poutine, coating all the fries and cheese yet not pooling at the bottom of the plate. All the right ingredients will only be as good as how they are put together. Cheese must be sprinkled on the fries as soon as they come out of the fryer. Gravy should be kept very warm and added right after the cheese. The poutine should then be served immediately. No making orders ahead of time and sticking them under a heat lamp, as this leads to very sad results. Our clientele understands this and will wait patiently to be able to wrap their hands around fresh poutine assembled just for them."

I knew that the only component of poutine left was the cheese. And I told Dene that I had always heard that the only true way to serve poutine was by using cheese curds.

"You'd really be surprised, Chuck, how different that is. Especially here at Titus Mountain. While we do offer cheese curds as a poutine option, most people order it with diced mozzarella cheese on the top. We have many great local cheese companies in the North Country, so no matter which form we get it in, it is always excellent. But it is true; most people order it with the mozzarella instead of curds."

I think Dene could sense my surprise at this revelation.

"Well, I can tell you this. We get huge crowds of skiers from Canada. And they order their poutine with diced mozzarella cheese on it by a ten to one margin over cheese curds. And they ought to know," he said. "Opinions regarding one or the other are strongly held, however. Much like religion or politics, it doesn't take much to get a spirited discussion started, if you really want to do that."

I asked Dene if he was as mystified as I was about how regionally closeted this food dish was. I told him that I had never seen it on a menu around my home in Central New York. It is just so North Country, isn't it?

"True, it is. I was born in the North Country and then left this area for about thirty years. Wherever I went I would mention poutine to people and they would look at me like I was crazy. So yes, I guess it is our little secret."

So if you ever get a hankering for a perfect portion of poutine and you just can't put your hands on your passport, well, there is a nice little family ski resort in Malone that has a plate of it waiting for you with your name on it—and it will be made fresh to order just for you!

Region Seven

CATSKILLS/HUDSON VALLEY

*Delaware, Greene, Ulster, Sullivan, Columbia, Dutchess,
Putnam, Westchester, Orange, Rockland*

24

CANDY CANES

Kingston

*E*verybody dreams about the corner candy store that was their favorite when they were a kid. Well, here is a dream come true. And it really is on a corner.

Mike Briglia is the Catskill Mountains Candy Cane King. He has owned his own corner candy store since 1980. "The original owner, Mike Altamarie, established this candy business back in 1917," he told me during a recent visit to the store. "I'd already been in the candy business, albeit a much smaller one, and I wanted to purchase this shop. Mr. Altamarie was getting up in his years, so one day I made him an offer and he accepted. He only had one requirement to finalize the sale. He insisted that all his candy recipes remain the same. And they have for nearly a century now."

Very little has changed in the way Mike makes his candy, especially his famous candy canes. "All of the equipment we use is original to Mr. Altamarie. He bought it on the Jersey shore. It was used to make taffy. He just refitted it to make candy canes.

"We keep it in good shape and it does its job for us. Every candy cane that we make has our own personal touch to it. We mix it, cook it, extrude it, twist it, cut it, flavor it and package it ourselves. Every single cane is hand twisted. The candy comes out in one long strip which is then cut into various sizes with a large set of snipping shears. People think, 'Oh, candy canes! What a fun business.' Well, it is fun, but it is also a lot of hard work."

I asked Mike about his early days at the corner shop. "Mr. Altamarie agreed to stay on for two years to show me the ropes. He was a tough

The Catskill Mountains Candy Cane King.

perfectionist. One day, at the beginning, he looked me up and down real good. He asked me if I knew what I was getting into. At that point Mr. Altamarie leaned over and picked up a hundred-pound bag of sugar, threw it on his shoulder and walked over and slammed it down on the baker's table. He was eighty-five years old at the time. He then turned to me and said, 'Let's see you do that,'" he laughed.

"Well, I did it. Barely."

Mike has been slinging giant bags of sugar over his shoulders for more than thirty years. He is now relegated to a wheelchair due to a bout with multiple sclerosis, but that hasn't slowed him down much. I asked him about heaving the bags of sugar today.

"It takes me a little longer, but I can still do it," he smiled as he raised and lowered his electric wheelchair. "We go through more than a ton of sugar here every two weeks."

The kitchen at Michael's Candy Corner is economical and very clean. Lots of white back there. They cook their candy canes in big copper pots over an open flame. "That's what sets us apart," he winked.

So how did the legend of the Candy Cane King really get its start?

"It is one of those stories that is just unbelievable," he began. "Several years ago I was in my shop here making candy canes for the holidays. It was busy but nowhere near what it is today. It was mid-October. I got a phone call from the Kingston Holiday Inn. They had a bus group at the hotel that needed something to do. Forty women who were supposed to take a Hudson cruise couldn't because it got rained out. The manager of the hotel asked me if he could send the group down to my shop to watch me make candy canes. He really needed something for these ladies to do.

"I had never done something like this before. But I told him, if the group would be patient with us, we would gladly welcome them to come in and observe our candy cane making operation. It was just me and another guy.

"So, the group comes in and we are in the back twisting and cutting the canes and telling our story and soon it was time for them to leave. One woman asked if she could take a couple of photos. I said, 'Of course.' Little did I know," he whispered.

At this point in Mike's story, he edged up close to me and prepared me. "You're not going to believe this, Chuck."

"That woman in the tour group, the one who took the pictures, turned out to be a reporter for the New York Times. Shortly after her visit I got a call to get the newspaper. And there it was—a full page article, with my photo in it, of our candy cane business. You can only imagine what happened next. Our phone went crazy. All the major newspapers in the country began calling for our story and people came flooding into our shop. It was unbelievable," he said as he shook his head.

I said how lucky he was to get so much free advertising from one newspaper article.

"That isn't even the story," he said with a smile. "After the *New York Times* ran that article we got a call from Better Homes and Gardens magazine, and they came to do a photo shoot. In December of 2002, my very own candy canes were featured on the cover of a magazine with a subscription of more than forty million readers. Things have never been the same since."

Mike Briglia is a rare artisan. They just don't make them like him anymore. His candy canes are the best you will find, whether the *New York Times* ever discovered him or not. He makes 250,000 canes a year from this little corner store. All handmade.

"The largest maker of candy canes in the world is a company called Bob's Candies. A few years back I attended a candy show in New York. I had my canes out for all the world to see. All of a sudden, who comes up but the head guy from Bob's. I was thrilled that he took some of my canes but never thought that I would ever hear from him again.

"Wouldn't you know it but a short time later I got a call from Bob, and he said he really enjoyed my candy canes. He told me that my canes were the most beautiful, unimaginable candy canes he'd ever seen. I told him I was quite shocked to hear that from the man who makes the most candy canes in the world. I told him I was just a little guy who makes three thousand candy canes a day, and he must make thirty thousand candy canes a day, so it was quite an accolade."

"So what did the tycoon candy maker say to that?" I asked.

"Well, there was silence at the end of the phone for a minute and then Bob said, 'Mike you are a great candy maker but you don't have a clue. We make *three million* candy canes a day,'" he laughed.

Mike's candy store also sells handmade chocolates, truffles, and other specialty items. But it is the candy canes that really put this cheerful Willie Wonka on the map. Mike has an elfin quality about him. Sparkling eyes and a ready smile. He seems to be in the perfect business for his personality.

"You know, I come rolling in here every morning with my cup of coffee just ready for the phone to ring. And when it does, it is usually somebody in the middle of nowhere saying, 'I want to order some of your candy canes.' How wonderful is that? I love it here. This is what I do. Every time I cut a candy cane there is a smile somewhere. It's kind of like I am everybody's Secret Santa."

So who, out there in the middle of nowhere, has been calling lately?

"Well, let's see," he said as he rustled through a pile of orders. "Here is one," he said as he handed it to me. Inside the envelope was a check and a letter from Fox Television Studios ordering up a couple of cases of Mike's candy canes to hand out on their popular sitcom *Raising Hope.*

"See, now we are even going to be on a hit television show," the candy maker said with a chuckle.

Region Eight

CAPITAL DISTRICT/SARATOGA

Albany, Rensselaer, Schenectady, Saratoga, Washington

25

SARATOGA CRACKERS

Saratoga

*W*ho knew a cracker could be so elegant?

"We take special pride in our crackers. Nothing but the best. And that goes to the packaging, also," Teresa Alger, the owner of Saratoga Crackers, told me. "Every package of crackers, about twenty in each, is hand packed in a shiny clear bag. Our label, created by our daughter, is a custom design that is classy and nostalgic of old Saratoga. My family has horses and my father is a retired racehorse jockey, so all of the images on our labels are actual photographs of my own horses, and one is of my dad racing his horse. The labels really speak to Saratoga's racing heritage. And we finish it all off by tying each bag together with an elegant black ribbon," she said.

Alger is the dynamic force behind these soon-to-be-well-established Saratoga icons. While you have met many other long established Upstate foods in this book—some that have been around for more than a century—Saratoga Crackers is the newest entry on our food favorite list.

"I've always been a baker," Teresa said. "Years ago, I was looking for a better, tastier, and healthier snack for my children to nibble on other than the junk food in the stores. I started out experimenting with these crackers. Before long, my family and friends heard about my crackers and encouraged me to let the general public know about them. We dubbed them Saratoga Crackers because we live here and bake here and we began taking baby steps out into the food world. That was back in 2007. I never expected the response to be so overwhelming. Everybody just loves our crackers," she said with a twinkle in her eye.

Owner Teresa Alger is seen here with two of her favorite passions: Saratoga Crackers and her beautiful horse Tater.

Although Saratoga Crackers are not yet sold in major supermarkets, that day is soon at hand. "We have had so many stores ask us to sell our crackers with them. We just want to be ready. I know that day is coming, but we want to make sure that we are prepared for the mass baking that it will require and that we do not lose our personal, homey touch."

As of now, Saratoga Crackers are sold at numerous outdoor markets, street festivals, farmers markets, and special events. "We get calls to bring our crackers from all over New York. We have just started getting exposure in New York City. We are now at a Brooklyn market two Sundays a month, where we always sell out. We even have started going to Connecticut to sell our crackers. We don't mind spending the night if we have to. We just want everybody to know about our product."

Teresa, who calls herself the Cracker Master, oversees every step of the production of her product. "It is all about health. We have a wide variety of cracker flavors, nearly twenty in all, but I insist that we maintain the healthy integrity of each cracker. We use no soy, no preservatives, no butter, and no additives. We use only extra virgin olive oil, no sugar, no trans fats. Each cracker is hand cut, so no two are alike. Our flavors include only the finest ingredients. It is all about taste and health. And you know what, Chuck? Many have told us that we make the absolute best tasting cracker they have ever had."

The flavor combinations are kaleidoscopic. I asked the Cracker Master what some of the favorites are. Her eyes lit up as she reached into her big tote and started to reveal bag after elegant bag of exquisite looking crackers.

"By far our top seller is Saratoga Spice and Parmesan, which includes our secret spices with a dash of red cracked pepper. They are a beautiful cracker that really looks great on a serving table or paired with a nice red wine. Some people even put a little slice of tomato or some herbs on them to make mini-bruschettas. They are our signature cracker. We also have a really nice Rosemary and Olive cracker. Our Sugar and Cinnamon cracker is a nice sweet treat, and for those looking for a healthy vegan snack this is one for them. Our Sea Salt cracker was our first one and is still very popular. We also have a Beer and Cheddar cracker which does very well. No store bought 'shake cheese' for that cracker. I hand grate the cheese from an aged wheel of cheddar. They really all sell well. We have something for everyone."

I asked Teresa if she had a personal favorite of the cracker varieties. "I really like the Mocha-Spresso cracker. We use the raw cacao nib, which is the best part of any chocolate, and espresso beans. My absolute two favorite flavor pairings are in our Raspberry and White Chocolate cracker. We use my own homegrown organic raspberries and we make our own white chocolate. I used to make scones out of these flavors. Now I say these are my scones made into a cracker," she laughed.

Teresa's energy and enthusiasm is contagious. Saratoga Crackers are a direct reflection of her standards. She is committed to a high-quality item, has her priorities all in order, and is ready to expand her business in the near future.

"Our whole family is involved in Saratoga Crackers. My family always comes first. And healthy foods, my customers, and my friends. Oh, and my horses, too," she smiled.

Teresa told me that all of her children are involved in the family business to a certain degree. I asked her what the youngest, just thirteen years old, did. "Oh, he is my very own cracker critic," she said.

I asked her, "How did you ever get a kid to try a Rosemary and Olive cracker?"

"He loved it!" she said with a hearty laugh.

26

PIE À LA MODE
Cambridge

*O*ne of the great joys of doing my series of Upstate books for Syracuse University Press is the amazing discoveries I find while making a routine turn on an old country back road. Like coming upon little Cambridge, New York, the birthplace of pie à la mode.

The Cambridge Hotel was once one of the swankiest hotels within a hundred miles. It is said that its comfort features, excellent service standards and fine dining were even with or above the glitziest Gilded Age palaces of nearby Saratoga. Tucked away in a small village in rural Washington County, the hotel towers above all the other buildings in town. Its signature feature is the distinctive three-story profile it cuts, anchored by a wraparound veranda. It once had a grand ballroom and exquisitely appointed guest rooms.

The story goes that in the 1880s, a well-heeled customer, Professor Charles Townsend, ordered a slice of the restaurant's apple pie to be adorned with a scoop of fresh vanilla ice cream. Served together. On the same dish.

Shocking.

This had never been done before. In fact, it was the newness, the sheer brashness of the delicacy that got it its moniker, pie à la mode (*à la mode* is French for "in the modern style").

Over the years there have been debunkers to this story, as is the case with so many other murky lineages of famous foods (see chapter 36 on the hamburger, for example). But the hotel steadfastly stuck to its pie crust and

The Cambridge Hotel was once one of the grandest in the Saratoga area. And while its famous dessert lives on, even a hit reality show couldn't save the hotel.

once and forever declared itself the birthplace of the rules-shattering new dessert, pie à la mode.

Of course, now you can order this dessert at virtually every restaurant in the country. Perhaps even in the world.

The regal hotel soldiered on for more than a century before the gilt started to fall off its edges. A common witch's brew presented a series of obstacles for many a rural business in the 1950s and 1960s. The hotel fell victim to newer, sleeker overnight accommodations nearby, high gasoline prices (the death knell to so many out-of-the-way places in rural locales), and high taxes.

Recently, as the death rattle of what once was a grand Victorian lady started echoing off the walls of the three dilapidated floors of the Cambridge Hotel, television food superstar Chef Gordon Ramsey was called in to put the paddles to this famous, dying patient.

Ramsey chose the Cambridge Hotel for his popular *Hotel Hell* series, in which he rides in to save the day for some poorly managed and failing hotel. Ramsey and his crew filmed for several days at the hotel. The threadbare rooms were updated, the woebegone dining hall was modernized, the staff was retrained, and the hotel's claim to fame, pie à la mode, was once again made the center of attentions.

And it all worked. Briefly.

After a short, successful spasm, the Hotel Cambridge finally died of natural causes. It became one of Chef Ramsey's rare failures. The shuttered historic hotel was auctioned off to the highest bidder (a local bank) for $299,000. The doors were closed forever on June 12, 2012, two months *before* the already-taped *Hotel Hell* episode aired on August 13, 2012.

RIP Cambridge Hotel. But thanks for the pie à la mode!

When I later visited this pretty little village, I wandered around peering into the tall empty windows of the hotel. There was very little to see. Doors were locked. Windows were draped. A Charlie Brown–style Christmas tree was situated in the front window. Yes, it was lit. Maybe for the entertainment of the four-year-old ghost known as Alice, who reportedly died at the hotel in 1913 and, well, has remained ever young there since.

The bones of the old building look remarkably sturdy and definitely worthy of a second go-round. The veranda, supported by a dozen three-story-tall fluted columns, looks positively inviting. Perhaps a nice relaxing spot to enjoy a piece of pie à la mode.

After exploring what I could of the Cambridge Hotel I strolled around this cute little village to see what else it offers. Next door to the Cambridge Hotel is the massive and magnificent 1903 Rice Mansion Inn and Carriage House. Jerome Rice owned the second-largest seed company in America, and when work was finished on his mansion he invited the entire town to come see his home. More than four hundred attended the open house.

At the beginning of the twenty-first century it was a fully restored twelve-room mansion bed and breakfast. Sadly, it too was "closed and in transition" on the day I visited the village. I can only imagine the day when these two side-by-side properties are up and fully operational again—what an engine of economic wellness for this little corner of Washington County they will be. The pairing of the birthplace of pie à la mode right next door to "the mansion built by seeds" will be formidable. A myriad of coffee shops, antique stores, and mom-and-pop businesses line both sides of the quaint Victorian downtown area.

As I drove out of town, about a mile on a secondary road, I passed a curious sign that just compelled me to stop.

"The Nuns of New Skete: New Skete Kitchens. Open Today."

Since no building was in sight, I turned up a gravel road and eventually came to a beautiful monastery tucked in the pines. The New Skete Nuns formed their monastery in 1969 here in Cambridge, just down the road from the monastery built by the Monks of New Skete. They are all members of the Byzantine-Rite Franciscan order. The brothers raise, train, and breed prized German shepherd puppies. They have written several books about their efforts, which have received international acclaim.

The sisters make cheesecakes.

The sign on the door said "Open," although no cars could be seen. What I did see inside was amazing.

A small welcome room greets you. It was bathed in muted colors, indirect lighting, and appointed with beautiful religious icons. It was like a little chapel.

Oh, and it also had one very large double door freezer.

Since nobody was around, I opened up the freezer to take a peek. Inside were some of the most beautiful homemade cheesecakes I have ever seen. All flavors. All in boxes with the prices printed on them. I looked around and still didn't see anyone. A note directed you to "Put your purchase money in a small box and to make out any checks to the Nuns of New Skete." I was chagrined to see a sign that read, "Due to the misuse of our services by some, please know that you are being videotaped."

All of a sudden a woman emerged from behind a religious statue and gently asked if she could help me. She was a baker at the monastery and told me that a large group of nuns was in the back making their world famous cheesecakes as we spoke. Unfortunately, she told me, I would be unable to interview or photograph them at work. They make thousands of cheesecakes throughout the year to support their monastic lifestyle and their charitable efforts. I tried one, and I can tell you it was spectacular.

It was a completely pleasing and surprising occurrence to meet up with the delightful Nuns of New Skete. I told one of them I was going to mention them in my book. She blushed. What a satisfying distraction I had found on a back road in rural Upstate New York, just a few miles from the Vermont border.

And the cheesecake was a bonus. All it was missing was a scoop of ice cream.

You know, cheesecake à la mode!

27

MINI HOT DOGS

Troy

*I*t didn't take long for the all-American hot dog to work its way up and off the Coney Island boardwalk and root itself in the small cities and towns of Upstate New York.

But something happened on the trip north. The hot dog underwent a transformation of sorts.

This chapter is about the unique configurations you can find in our region when you go looking for a hot dog. Up here you will find white hots, grillers, Michigans, mini-dogs, Hofmann's hots, Tobin's First Prizers, and Texas hots slathered with Greek sauce. Hot dog variations? We've got them. Hot dog franchises? Not so much.

One of the first big hot dog franchises in the United States (and there are still not many) was Lum's, an Upstate place that served a frank soaked in beer. Not your typical family fare, eh? I remember going to Lum's back in the black-and-white days of my youth. We'd stop for lunch at one near Lake George on our way to vacation. My dad would nose our big blue Ford Country Squire station wagon into a too-small parking spot, and all ten members of my family would pile out and head into Lum's for lunch.

I distinctly remember the sign heralding their famous "hot dogs steamed in beer" headliner. None of my seven siblings or I was old enough to drink beer, of course, so there was always something a little dangerous about these fat, sweaty hot dogs, which would arrive at our table with a slightly pungent aroma to them. We'd all sneak a bite when our parents were not looking, and I thought maybe I got a little buzzed on them in the process. And if so, what about dear old Dad? I wondered, as we piled back

The mini hot dogs from Famous Lunch have been shipped around the world.

into our boat-sized vehicle, if he was OK to drive after eating one of these edgy sandwiches. I mean could he be pulled over for DWUIHD: driving while under the influence of a hot dog?

Just after college I worked at another doomed fast food place (at least for our area) that sold hot dogs, the Germanic-themed Der Weinerschnitzel. It was on State Street in Schenectady. They made me an assistant manager. The year was about 1969, and Der Weinerschnitzel was one of the first fast food delis that utilized microwave ovens.

The ovens were very new at the time and this particular franchise jumped on the band wagon and zapped everything they made in the microwave before serving it. I clearly remember that this was probably not a good way to serve up a hot dog as they popped and exploded in the little atomic ovens and the buns became rock hard.

Baseball Hall of Famer Reggie Jackson and country music star Roy Clark were early schnitzel shills. Eventually they dropped the "der" and became just Weinerschnitzel. I left the company before a year was out and the franchise continues on, now mostly centered in the West, with more than a dozen restaurants in the Los Angeles area alone.

So while you may find a franchise around that serves up a good traditional hot dog (like Johnny Rockets, for example) there are not nearly as many as serve up the good old hamburger.

But if you want something a little different, a little odd in your hot dog world, well, welcome to Upstate New York.

The Michigan hot dogs of far northern New York are still a mystery fifty years after people started eating them. You can only find them within about a one-hundred-mile radius of Plattsburgh. And nobody really knows how they got their name. A Michigan is your basic steamed frank on a steamed bun. The sauce, a close companion to the traditional Greek meat sauce found elsewhere, is a little heavier on the mustard side. This is a substantial sized hot dog ("red hot") in a natural casing.

If you have a hankering for a Michigan you might have to time your appetite with the seasons. Although some year-round places serve this decidedly northern New York dog, several of the most well-known places close during the hard-bitten winters that are the hallmark of the Platts-burgh area. Gus's Red Hots and Clare and Carl's, both in Plattsburgh, are two old standbys.

Clare and Carl's closes at the beginning of November, and since they realize they will be depriving their steady fan base of their beloved Michigan's for about a half year, they sell them for just a buck a piece on their final day and also offer up their Michigan sauce in pint jars to carry everybody through the winter. Don't be fooled by the big red neon sign that says Texas Red Hots on top of the small ten-stool eatery. Everybody inside calls them Michigans.

At Gus's on the other side of town they serve Michigans, but everybody calls them red hots. Go figure. Gus's is a more traditional sit-down diner with table and counter service and an expanded menu. It is important to note that at both places you can get Glazier hot dogs. These bright red "snap back at you" hot dogs are unique to the North Country and are made in Malone, an hour west of Plattsburgh.

Around Liverpool, just outside of Syracuse, when you are talking about going out to grab a hot dog, chances are you are heading over to Heid's. This legendary Upstate *Happy Days*–style drive-in is one of the most popular eating places in the region. They are also one of the oldest continuously run drive-in stands in America, having opened in 1917.

Heid's is classic old school. The building design features flashing neon signs, round retro windows, bright striped awnings, and all the other trappings of the fast food drive-ins of our youth (or of our dreams).

The specialty here is the Hofmann Coneys and Franks. Hofmann franks are the premier hot dog of Upstate New York. Frank Hofmann, a German butcher, arrived in Syracuse in 1861 to open a meat market. By the time his two sons took over in 1879, Hofmann's product was already touted as America's Greatest Hot Dog. McDonald's hamburgers have nothing on Hofmann hot dogs. Well maybe a little. Hofmann trumpets the fact that they have sold over *one hundred million* hot dogs since founder Frank Hofmann first sharpened a carving knife in his shop in the Salt City.

One of Upstate's most unique contributions to the hot dog culture is the mini-dog. Nobody knows where they came from, how they got started, why some call them Texas hots and yet top them with Greek sauce, or even why New York's Capital District is home to some of America's most venerable and popular mini-doggeries.

I was first introduced to these mostly greasy spoon delicacies in my college days in Albany. There has always been a real connection between Albany and this concoction, started by Greek immigrants a century ago. I used to haunt a place called Johnny's Hot Dogs located near where Western and Central Avenues join and morph into State Street. It was run by a big garrulous man with thick Coke-bottle glasses and a hard-to-pronounce Greek last name. He was a friendly-giant sort of a guy, despite the small handgun peeking out of his waistband or hidden under the counter. I first started going there in 1967 and was a steady customer for several years.

Johnny's mini-dogs would roll around and around on his warmer in the window until somebody ordered some. And I do mean *some*. Nobody ever ordered just one. In fact, it was not unheard of for me to make a visit and order up a half dozen after swimming or playing squash at the nearby Albany YMCA. Johnny's Greek sauce was spicy, meat laden, and had just enough of a grease quotient to it to make it irresistible.

Steven Wade, now a Dean's Executive Professor at Santa Clara University in California, recently spoke with me about his memories of working at Johnny's.

"Johnny's was my place of employment for two years at college in Albany in 1969 and 1970. I worked every Friday and Saturday night there. The place was not particularly distinctive for its cuisine; we served hot dogs, lemon meringue pie, coffee and soda. Probably something else but I don't remember.

"The clientele was more interesting to a nineteen-year-old from Sidney, New York, than the food. Hot dogs were twenty cents and a soda and coffee were fifteen. A lady who cleaned offices in Albany in the evening came in with her young son every Friday around 9:00 a.m. She ordered a hot dog for each of them, a coffee for her, and a soda for him. They split a piece of pie. She paid with a dollar and told me to keep the change.

"The hot dogs were most distinctive for their price, twenty cents. There were none cheaper. We grilled them on parallel warming rods, about fifty at a time. Freihofer buns were kept in a steam drawer below the grill. Condiments were on the counter in back except for a mysterious 'Greek sauce' that was in a warm vat next to the dogs. This sauce may have been the unique draw at one time, but during my tenure there the price was just as important.

"Johnny, the owner of this emporium, also owned a similar place in Latham and made his sauce for both in a huge pot. My memory of the sauce is that it was comprised of some meat, perhaps some lamb, and spices swimming in grease. People liked it a lot and some ordered dogs with every condiment, including sauerkraut and Greek sauce. Late at night we got orders for one or two dozen hot dogs, usually with the works. We loaded them on a paper tray, slathered on the sauce and condiments, and slipped them into a paper bag. It is hard to imagine what they looked like upon delivery, but the orders kept coming.

"Johnny's was not an exclusive eatery and was situated on Central Avenue so we had an everyday kind of crowd including many regulars. Because we were open so late and there were occasional holdups, we did what we could to entice Albany cops to enjoy endless dogs and bottomless coffee all pro bono. Many of the older customers remembered Legs Diamond, the famous gangster who was shot around the corner at 67 Dove Street back in the 1930s. A couple of bookies frequented the restaurant, too, but as far as I could tell never ate there.

"Johnny's was a colorful place if nothing else."

Remarkably, within a ten minute drive of each other just a couple miles north of the Capitol building itself you will find three places that have been selling these bite-sized wonders for a total of nearly two centuries. Hot Dog Charlie's, with three locations, is the oldest in the bunch. Again, it was a Greek immigrant named Strates Fentekes who opened up a shop in 1922 selling tiny hot dogs with his own homemade Greek sauce. Dubbed "Charlie" when his customers couldn't pronounce his real name, Fentekes was famous for his "hairy arm serve." He would line the mini-dogs up in a row on his hairy Greek forearm and then slather them with all the fixings one after another.

In 1954, Gus Haita opened up his eponymous shop, a small red walk-up window squashed among the working class homes on 25th Street in nearby Watervliet. They've been selling mini-dogs with homemade meat sauce from the front window ever since, and Gus's son, Steve, now runs this iconic Capital District institution. Both of Steve's folks, naturally, were Greek immigrants. Gus's Hot Dogs is the less frilly of the two places, but really both hot dog stands are bare-bones places where people with hearty appetites go and commonly start out their order by shouting, "Give me four originals, please."

Not to be outdone is Famous Lunch in Troy. And since, in all fairness, a lot of this book is about my own personal favorites, well frankly, this is it.

Famous started out as Quick Lunch back in 1932 at the same location it is in today. Scott Vasil is the owner, following in the footsteps of his father, Steve, now eighty-eight, and his uncles Chris and Nick Semon, all of whom were Greek immigrants.

So with this long line of Greek heritage, I asked Scott if he felt he was "into the hot dog born."

"Ha, not a chance," he chuckled. "Although I did work here as a kid, you know, coming in after school and washing dishes and such, I never thought I would end up owning Famous someday. I actually went to school right up the street and got an engineering degree at Rensselaer Polytechnic Institute.

"Unfortunately, when I got out there were not a lot of engineering jobs to be found, so I started getting more involved in the restaurant. At the time, the only ones left from the old days were my dad and my Aunt Kay (Uncle Nick's widow). So I thought I might just as well get in line. I took over the business in 1995, and we are still going strong."

I asked Scott whether he ever regrets not using his engineering degree.

"Well, this business certainly has its challenges, but I do enjoy it. Of course the people, my customers, always keep it interesting for me."

And so, after more than eighty years in business, I asked, "Who is your customer base?"

"Well, just like I did, many of the students at RPI right up the hill certainly like us. I mean, the hot dogs are only eighty-five cents, and that is with the works on them. So they love it. We get a lot of workers, business people, lawyers, politicians, and just folks from the neighborhood. We are kind of a tradition here in Troy."

There is a real sense of rejuvenation in this historic city on the Hudson River. The downtown area is bustling with construction and rehab projects turning old empty buildings into new eateries, galleries, and residential living spaces.

"Downtown Troy is alive," Scott said. "There is a lot of new and a lot of old. That mix really makes it unique. I mean, right around the corner they are putting up new condominiums and yet right next door to us is another restaurant, Manory's. It was started in 1913, right in the same spot, and is Troy's oldest continuously operating restaurant. So the new and old, we live together and it really works for Troy."

OK, so why mini-dogs?

"I really don't know," he laughed. "I mean they sure didn't eat them in Greece. But for some reason, many generations ago several different Greek families showed up in this area and started the tradition. We don't just sell a hot dog with sauce on it. There is a lot of thought that goes into our product.

"Our hot dogs are made special and are three-and-a-half inches long. Helmbold's makes them for us and always has. They are, I think, the oldest meat company in the area. They began in Troy over a hundred years ago. They make them for us using a mixture of beef, pork, and assorted natural spices. They are made with an all-natural casing.

"Hembold's is a Troy icon. In fact they used to have their butcher shop right out our back door. If we ran out of hot dogs they would just walk some over to us," he said. "Our buns are made by Bella Napoli Bakery, which is a top bakery in the Capital Region. They are kneaded dough rolls made perfectly to fit our Famous hot dogs. The sauce is a chewy, meat sauce with our own special spices in it. We use a Medford style mustard which is the original French's brand prepared mustard."

Once you get over the novel idea of eating four or five of these little finger-sized hot dogs in one sitting, it really all comes down to the sauce. "People just can't get enough of it. We call it our Zippy sauce, and we sell it by the jar also. It is a very big seller. In fact, we have one guy who buys it just to put on his spaghetti at home," Scott said.

"And of course because our hot dogs are so small everybody thinks they are Joey Chestnut or some kind of extreme eating champ. In fact, the record for the most hot dogs consumed in one sitting at Famous is thirty-nine dogs eaten by Scott Lovelace in 2010. A fraternity from RPI come in here once and ate 825 hot dogs at once. There were thirty-eight people from the FIJI Fraternity. That really kept our cooks busy," he told me.

I asked the newest generation of a long line of Greek hot dog artisans how it feels to be in charge of a family business that goes back almost a century.

"I do take great pride in Famous. We have been around a long time and people look to us for tradition. The *New York Times* and the *New York Post* and many other media outlets have come and interviewed us. It makes me so proud. It is just a little hot dog, but to me it means everything. When people visit their old stomping grounds back here in Troy, they always stop in for a quick hello and a Famous. And that is nice."

Scott shared with me a touching story about the cheeky name "World Famous," which is on their awning out front.

"True story, Chuck. In 1958, Corporal Gordon Gundrum, a Troy native, was stationed at the U.S. Embassy in Moscow. He had such a hankering for his hometown hot dogs that he actually arranged for KLM Royal Dutch Airlines to fly him some. He called it 'Operation Hot Dog,' and our hot dogs arrived just in time to be served to the U.S. Ambassador to Russia on his fifty-fourth birthday. The world press had a field day with that, and ever since we have called ourselves 'world famous' in his honor."

And that tradition still carries on.

Greg Miller, a Troy insurance agency owner, sends Famous hot dogs to soldiers all over the world. "They are amazed when these hot dogs show up," he told me. "I overnight them to the soldiers and they have sent back photos of them and their buddies eating them in all sorts of places. For these members of the military, some of them our wounded warriors, this is a nice little piece of home that really lifts their spirits.

"In fact not too long ago we had quite a bit of excitement here in Troy. A little girl, who actually grew up right next to me as a kid, is now a Brigadier General. She graduated from West Point and did two tours of duty in Iraq. Recently, she was named the first female to head the Arkansas National Guard. All of us in Troy are so proud of her. So I sent Brig. Gen. Trisha Anslow one hundred Famous hot dogs with the works to congratulate her."

I asked Greg if he heard from her that they arrived safely.

"Yes, and she said I could expect a photograph real soon of herself and all the other generals sitting around chowing down on Troy's own Famous hot dogs," he laughed.

ONE FOR THE HISTORY BOOKS

28

AMERICA'S LAST HOWARD JOHNSON'S RESTAURANT
Lake Placid

*I*n this book we meet a lot of firsts. The first time Teressa Bellissimo dragged a chicken wing through a bucket of hot sauce thereby creating a national bar food sensation in Buffalo back in 1964. The first time Pete Donnelly squeezed out a perfect chocolate and vanilla twist cone from his brand new 1953 Cherry-Burrell ice cream maker up in Saranac Lake (he still uses it). The first time the Caffè Aurora put some petit fours in their bakery shop window in Poughkeepsie and First Lady Eleanor Roosevelt pulled up in her limousine to buy them.

But this chapter of *A Taste of Upstate New York* doesn't take a look at a historic first. Instead, we take a look at a historic last.

The final orange-roofed Howard Johnson's restaurant in the country is in Lake Placid.

"My dad started the business after working for the original owners, the Brewster sisters, back in the mid-1950s," Mike Butler, the owner, told me. "I was in here at a very young age. In fact, I grew up right here under this orange roof. When I was five years old, my Dad placed me up on a milk crate and showed me how to butter the muffin pans," he chuckled.

The Howard Johnson's chain of restaurants was the largest in the United States during the 1960s and early 1970s. There were more than one thousand restaurants around the country, in every state of the union. The iconic orange roof, the twirling weathervane, and the image of Simple Simon and the Pie Man were as ubiquitous along the baby boom highways as Burma Shave signs.

Mike Butler is the owner of the last orange-roofed Howard Johnson's restaurant in America. Here he is standing next to his vintage delivery vehicle in the restaurant's parking lot in Lake Placid.

"Howard Johnson was a real person and a real genius," Butler said. "He invented children's menus, games to occupy kids, boiling bags, a standalone steak house (the Red Coach Grill), and the bar-in-the-middle pub style restaurant (the Ground Round). He basically invented clam strips and perfected the Friday fish fry. For his famous twenty-eight flavors of ice cream, he imported chocolate from Switzerland, fresh strawberries from California, and vanilla from South America. He hired the top fashion designer Christian Dior to create the waitress uniforms. Famed French pastry chef Albert Kumin came up with the HoJo's Danish pastry recipe, while internationally acclaimed chefs Jacques Pépin and Pierre Franey worked in the test kitchens churning out thousands of gallons of beef burgundy and scallops in mushroom sauce. Mr. Johnson was a real stickler for detail," Butler told me, "and that was why he was one of the most successful restaurateurs in America."

Times have changed since those heady days when families would pile into their block-long station wagons and head out for extended stay vacations.

"Like everything, what was new becomes old," the owner told me. "Over the years, the restaurant chain was swallowed up by bigger and bigger companies, and it lost all its identification. It still has its motor lodges, but the famous orange roofed 'Home of 28 Flavors' is long gone. Howard Johnson's hasn't even made their own ice cream in over twenty-five years. We are the last one with the famous roof. And you know what? People love that."

One other final Howard Johnson's restaurant is open part time in Bangor, Maine. It does not have the famous orange roof, though. Out of more than a thousand from the old days, if you want a taste of HoJo nostalgia, Lake Placid is the place to go.

"We still have our regulars for sure. But not many of the younger kids ever had the sentimental attachment to the restaurant that the older folks have. After Sunday church, our place fills up with locals. And once in a while a celebrity comes by like Jamie Farr from M*A*S*H or Willie Nelson or Gary Trudeau and his wife, Jane Pauley. When I was younger, I remember singer Kate Smith (a summer resident) coming in here every Sunday after mass and ordering a big stack of blueberry pancakes. Our lodge next door (Butler also owns the adjoining Comfort Inn motel) has housed many winter Olympians who come to Lake Placid to train. But nostalgia is what it is, and we are glad to be here to cater to customers who have been loyal to us for a very long time."

I asked Mike Butler what he thinks about when he comes in the morning and turns the lights on and flips over the Open sign. "I think about growing up in this place with my father. Howard Johnson's is part of my DNA. Back in the day, when the company was flourishing, it was pretty cool to work here. I remember unloading one hundred tubs of ice cream twice a day from the trucks. I spent all day long in the freezer on those days. But it was fun."

As I left, I asked Mike if he had any regrets about being the proprietor of a place whose fame and notoriety are firmly rooted in the past. "Not really. My dad worked hard to build this place up. He always told me 'great service plus great food at great prices' were the keys to success, and he was right. And I actually love it when some old timers come in here on vacation and ask if we still have fried clam strips like we did when they were kids. We do, of course" he said.

"Any other benefits to the whole nostalgia thing?" I asked.

"Yes. Just recently on the TV show *Mad Men*, the character Don Draper and his wife, Megan, talked about going on a client visit to Upstate New York to the Howard Johnson's. They went, ate in a Howard Johnson's booth, had our famous sherbet, and even had a fight in the parking lot with the orange roof in the background. Although the scene was actually filmed in Hollywood, the very next day our phones rang off the hook. People wanted to know if it was true that we were still here and open. Several major newspapers even called and interviewed me. So nostalgia certainly has a value," he smiled.

UPSTATE FOOD TRADITIONS

29

FARMERS MARKETS
Plattsburgh

*F*ood traditions grow on you. After a while you become so used to them you cannot even imagine where they started.

Upstate New York certainly hasn't been a pioneer in a lot of food traditions, but they have sure tried to perfect them. The farmers markets discussed in this chapter are similar to ones found around the country (and the world), but we put a special touch on them in Upstate.

Farmers markets? Or farm markets? There is a difference. The former features a group of sellers getting together in a shared space to sell their products. The farm market is pretty much the same thing, but it usually features just a single grower or farm family who has grown their business from a little stand to a permanent market. Both proliferate the Upstate region.

There was a time, in the 1930s for example, when the words "farmer's market" meant some farmer had dragged a little card table out to the roadside and piled it up with some sweet corn to sell. Usually on the honor system. In the post–World War II era of burgeoning suburbs, spreading shopping malls, and bigger and bigger supermarkets, moms bought all of their produce at the store. The big new A&P, or the Grand Union, Wegmans, Loblaws, or even Victory Markets. These destination shopping hubs featured big, shiny, mirrored produce cases loaded with forests of greens, mountains of melons, and bushels of red, ripe tomatoes. A mechanical arm moved back and forth overhead like a carnival game, misting the produce at regular intervals. We chose what we wanted, weighed the items ourselves, and then bagged our bounty and placed it in our overflowing

Ron Pray and his wife, Margaret, started their farm market fifty years ago in Plattsburgh. It is still going strong! (Photo courtesy of whitefacenewyork.com)

shopping carts. It was a new, healthy, and innovative way to shop. Who knew vegetables could be so much fun?

Upstaters have to look no farther than their downstate cousins to find the origins of today's farmers markets. Immigrants clogged the streets of the Lower East Side of Manhattan at the turn of the twentieth century. In Jewish and Italian neighborhoods, large numbers of vendors sold everything from onions to baked goods to sheep entrails from rickety carts and feeble stands set up along the squalid sidewalks of the city. Bargains could be found, haggling was a prerequisite, and disease was almost always a "silent participant" in this earliest form of a farmers market.

In the 1940s, Mayor Fiorello LaGuardia moved everybody off the filthy streets and into enclosed arcades that could hold hundreds of stalls, could be monitored for health concerns, and could be taxed to raise city revenue. One of the largest, the Essex Street Market, played host to nearly five hundred food venders in the early 1940s. The streets were quiet and cleaner, and the new farmers market was humming with business.

In bucolic Upstate, "the breadbasket of New York," our thousands of farm families ate what they produced, and if there was anything left over, well, out came the card table for Mom to make a little "going-to-town money." Like everything else, however, the times they were a-changin'.

Slowly the world of food consciousness turned, like a giant ship changing course. Health and fitness started to become something we actually practiced rather than just talked about. President John Kennedy put America on a treadmill and kicked us outdoors to get fit. He urged everybody to take a hike. And we did. Thousands all across the country, both young and old, took a fifty-mile hike in the name of the President's Council on Physical Fitness. Guys did deep knee bends while watching Jack LaLanne on television. Women did sensual stretching movements to the encouragement of the *Debbie Drake Show* (alright, so guys watched the *Debbie Drake Show*, too). Both became national fitness icons.

We started biking and hiking and running and just about everything else we could do to get fit and stay fit. Health magazine subscriptions soared, and image-conscious Hollywood demanded we strive to look like Mia Farrow and Elvis Presley. And, of course, a new spotlight was thrown on the food we ate.

Enter the farmers markets.

In the 1960s and 1970s, farmers were less and less content to just do the old card table routine. More and more, they loaded up the pickup truck with boxes and bushels and headed for the street corners of the towns and villages all across Upstate. And they brought more than just corn with them this time. The truck was filled with melons, apples, peas, rhubarb, potatoes, berries, and anything else they could plant, pull, and sell.

Soon farmers markets were sprouting up everywhere. Meat was added to the menu. And dairy. And pies and cakes. And homemade soaps and candles. And hand carved bird houses. Fresh flowers and herbs. And a live band playing in the background. And face painting for the kids. Slowly, from the crowded, steaming streets of turn-of-the-century Manhattan up to today, the concept of a farmers market has transformed the way we shop. Farm to table they call it. Bringing the country into the city. Buying local. Weekends now begin with a visit to the farmers market downtown to see your neighbors and buy some turnips.

Yes, in an ever so subtle way, the concept of selling food products from a homemade cart on the streets of the Lower East Side to today's health-conscious, family-friendly Upstate farmers markets took just about a century to evolve.

Clearly, Upstate New York did not invent the farmers market. Who did? Who knows? They have been around since ancient times after all. We have hundreds in our region. But we do have some very interesting farmers markets that I have been to and think you would like. Let me tell you about them.

The Windmill Farm and Craft Market in Penn Yan is one of the biggest and oldest farmers markets in Upstate. For approximately three decades, thousands have been meeting at this Finger Lakes crossroads to scoop up local food treats as well as craft items from the more than two hundred vendors. Crowds have surpassed ten thousand on some special event weekends at The Windmill. The shopping is so good that motor coach companies routinely route their tour buses here for a stop.

The Lake Placid Farmers Market offers a stunning array of food items for sale. Despite its chilly location (or perhaps because of it), dozens of North Country farmers and vendors ply this market with enough usual and unusual fruits and vegetables to meet even the pickiest of chefs' requirements. I mean, who would have ever thought you could shop for fresh kohlrabi, tomatillos, Chinese greens, or okra here in the shadow of Whiteface Mountain?

The Capital District is home to two of my favorites. The Troy Farmers Market takes place on one of the most delightful streets Upstate has to offer. River Street sidles along next to the Hudson River and displays a myriad of amazing architectural marvels and historic sites at every corner. The farmers market spreads out right under the massive ninety-foot-tall Soldiers and Sailors Monument to Rensselaer County men who served in the Civil War. All along River Street, which has been called one of the most well-preserved nineteenth-century downtown avenues in America, vendors are tent pole to tent pole selling homemade food, artisan crafts, and art work. Thousands come through each weekend in the summer to enjoy this wonderful taste of Troy.

Across the Hudson in Menands you will find perhaps the granddaddy of all of Upstate's farmers markets. The venerable Capital District Farmers Market has been in existence since 1933. It is still an old-time, no-frills marketplace, and the supply of goods here is really incredible. Huge cuts of local pasture-fed beef, handfuls of dry roasted nuts, dozens of whoopee pies, hundreds of bushels of fruit, and thousands of bowers of flowers. Huge throngs come each week for a great breakfast, to sample some fine New York State wines, or just to immerse themselves in the nostalgic feeling that washes over you when you visit this sprawling farmers market that is still in the same place it was when FDR began his first term!

While geographically poles apart, there are two other markets that people seem to love (and vote for in the ubiquitous "best of" polls). One is in the lower Hudson Valley and the other is along the St. Lawrence Seaway Trail. One is a farmers market that takes place where the highway meets the dirt road just north of New York City. And the other is a very, very special family farm market that wears its heart on its sleeve in Platts-burgh. You should try them both. Hey, what's a little 289-mile one-way road trip?

The Pleasantville Farmers Market is located in the historic little village that is home to *Reader's Digest* magazine (how Norman Rockwell is that?). It is an hour's drive north of Times Square to just about where you start to feel the macadam slip away and the dirt road start to manifest itself. More than fifty vendors attend this weekend party, and a large number of upscale shoppers (yes, many from metropolitan New York) come to buy the harvest's bounty of fruits, vegetables, baked goods, locally produced beer and wine, Hudson Valley hard cider, and more. This farmers market really has an eye on making the weekends lively by providing an energetic and eclectic lineup of performers who keep the downtown Memorial Plaza site bouncing along every weekend from May to November.

About as far away from Pleasantville as you can get (almost six hours north as the crow flies) you will come to my favorite farm market in Upstate. Pray's Farm Market in Plattsburgh has been going steadily now for over a half century. Everything they sell in this onetime road stand is grown by the Pray family. Everybody from miles around comes here, and they have been coming since the 1960s. It is about as close to a tradition in the North Country as you can get.

It is, in a word, special.

"I was born on a farm down in Keeseville where my folks planted 110 acres," Ron Pray, eighty, told me. "We used to haul a bunch of fruits and vegetables out to the side of the road and sell them. People seemed to like everything, so in 1965 a place came up for sale in Plattsburgh. We bought it and made the move," he said. "It was an old house on a two lane country road. The first thing we did was take a chain saw to the house, cut out the walls and put in our farm market. Been here ever since," he laughed.

Ron's family continues to run this little slice of heaven on the far edge of Upstate New York. He and his wife, Margaret, had four sons who grew up at the farm market. "Once they hit six years old we put them to work," he told me. "And believe it or not, they are all still here, with their wives and a bunch of grandchildren all helping out."

You can tell Ron misses Margaret, who passed away a couple of years ago. "She was right beside me all the way for fifty-three and a half years," he said quietly. But the market keeps him busy, and the growing Pray family works right along with the elder grower of the bunch. Ron still keeps the family farm down in Keeseville where they grow everything they sell at the family market in Plattsburgh, fifteen miles away.

"Our most popular items of course are the corn and tomatoes. We grow 30,000 tomato plants every year, 40 acres of corn, and 10 acres of strawberries. We have five large greenhouses where we grow 8,000 hanging baskets. It keeps us busy. Real busy," he said. "Our motto is 'Try the rest, and then come for the best. You be the judge!'"

Ron was a prison guard at the Clinton Correctional Facility in nearby Dannemora for nearly twenty years. "I had to get out because I had heart problems," he told me. "Glad I did too. This is where I belong. With my little farm market and my family."

Like I said. Pray's Farm Market is a very, very special place.

30

ICE CREAM STANDS

Saranac Lake

*T*here are many harbingers of summer in Upstate New York.

The drive-in theaters open up (if you can find one; of the once more than two hundred there are now fewer than two dozen), out-of-state license plates start snaking up Route 28 to the Baseball Hall of Fame in Cooperstown, the black flies return to the Adirondacks, Lowes and Home Depot run out of patio furniture for sale, demolition derbies at county fairs become the central rallying point for teenagers across a wide swath of the region, the cool and clear swimming holes from the Gunks to the Finger Lakes are packed with bathers seeking refuge on days where the temperature creeps above the eighty-degree mark, and ice cream stands begin opening all over the place like wild flowers popping into bloom on a crisp, Upstate spring day.

There were plenty of places to get your ice cream cones back in the day. And all of them were wonderful. With old standbys like Stewarts Shops, Tastee Freeze, Perry's, Dairy Queen, and Carvel, Upstate had a galaxy of frozen choices when it came time to scream for ice cream.

And don't forget the tantalizing siren's song of the ubiquitous Mister Softee trucks crawling through our neighborhoods looking for hungry, sweaty kids to entice. There is now an army of more than six hundred of these jingle-bell-belting, refrigerated ice cream mirages appearing on small town streets every day.

Ice cream stands are popular throughout the country, but our vivid memories of these stands in Upstate make them a unique summertime memory for all of us. Many had slanted roofs, giant papier- mâché ice

Donnelly's ice cream stand in Saranac Lake is so small, only five customers can be inside at one time.

cream cones on top, banners flapping in the wind screaming out the ever-growing number of flavors, and of course those garish yellow neon bug bulbs that lit the way for you and your family on a muggy summer evening.

Funny. I don't ever remember those bug bulbs working, do you? I remember countless times standing at the pick-up window waiting for my hard-shell dipped chocolate cone, staring up at the B-movie sized spiders webbing their way from bulb to bulb as an armada of moths churned the thick air with their silky wings.

In the small towns and villages of Upstate, these little stands are communal gathering places to swap gossip and check up on old friends. Ice cream habits are formed, favorites are settled on, and patterns emerge. I spoke with Emily Hull, the longtime manager of Mac-A-Doodles on Main Street in Stamford, a village known as the Queen of the Catskills. She told me that trends are common at these places, and they are easy to spot.

"After working here for years I can almost tell you what a person is going to order just by their age," she said. "For example, the littlest kids will usually start with just a vanilla until they get used to the flavor. Maybe with a coating of colored sprinkles on it. Kids from four to twelve usually go for the crazy names on the flavors, so you can bet they are going to opt for Blue Goo or Mint-Ting-A-Ling. Older teens are harder to predict so they are usually all over the place."

I asked her about adults and seniors. "Middle-aged women go for the dramatic, romantic names like Raspberry Truffle or Bittersweet Symphony (coffee with dark chocolate). Men in this same age group stick with anything chocolate. The seniors from say fifty on up are the easiest. They are set in their ways and almost never change. If a man has been ordering a maple walnut ice cream cone since he was in his forties, you can bet he isn't going to switch now that he is in his seventies. We have some of these regulars at Mac-A-Doodles, and we start making the cone for them before they even say anything," she laughed.

See what I mean about patterns?

It's odd, but when I think about these ice cream stands, which I have been patronizing for more than six decades, I never once remember having a bad experience at any of them. Unlike steak houses or spaghetti places or sushi bars, which can be hit-or-miss, an ice cream stand never disappoints. Sure, some are more memorable than others, but usually it is not because of the ice cream quality but more because of the emotional immersion one goes through when pulling up on a steamy night with a car full of hungry kids. You wade through the mass of bugs (which are smugly ignoring the bug lights, of course) and order up a cone. Just a plain old ice cream cone. It is tall, frosty, tasty, cheap, and simple. You are hot and perspiring. It just all comes together at that little sliding serving window. It works.

Like I said, it never disappoints.

Upstate's summer ice cream stands have crazy, creative, carnival midway–style names and themes. The scarf-wearing man of snow atop a red-and-white-striped awning beckons you to The Snowman ice cream stand in Troy. The Crooked Lake Ice Cream Parlor sits just a block off Keuka Lake, which has been known as the crooked lake because of its off-kilter shoreline for as long as anybody can remember. Why is there a man-eating shark eating an ice cream cone up on the sign at the intersection of Routes 5 and 20 in Bloomfield? Right. You are at Shark's Ice Cream. And yes,

Jolly Cow Ice Cream in Lake Katrine not only shows a happy bovine on its sign but also features a life-size black and white right in the parking lot for kids to climb on while waiting for their ice cream.

Some ice cream stands reach mythic proportions, both on longevity and legacy. Folks in the Capital District will tell you that the only true sign that Old Man Winter has released his frozen hold on the area is the opening of the famed Kurver Kreme on Central Avenue. Punxatawney has a ground hog. Albany has an ice cream stand. And the stand has been around over fifty years, a lot longer than that wishy-washy rodent down in Pennsylvania.

Every time I walk through the front door of Hoppie's in Oxford, I feel like I am entering Mr. Peabody's Wayback Machine. The quaint shop has been on the village green here for decades. Inside, it evokes memories of soda shops from the 1950s (and beyond). I invariably order a cone and a coke, settle in to a red-padded parlor seat, and begin to dump a fortune into the 1950s jukebox. For a guy my age, there is nothing quite like licking a Perry's hand-dipped strawberry cone while listening to Frankie Valli and the Four Seasons on an old Wurlitzer jukebox in Oxford. Sublime.

One of the amusing aspects of Upstate's ice cream stands and parlors is how they brag about their age. No, they are not shy about proclaiming to the world how old they are. The Kayuta Drive-In in Remsen, for example. Recently I stepped inside for a cone and had to virtually duck beneath a huge sign proudly shouting "Now in Our 50th Year." Yessir, they are old and, darn it, they want you to know about it.

It really is amazing when you think about it. For over five decades Kayuta has been sitting along Route 12 between Boonville and Remsen dispensing cones (and, now, other food items). When it opened in 1963, cars going by were few and far between. Then the Adirondacks became "Vacationland" with all of their little theme parks and motels, and traffic got busier. Route 12 has been widened several times, to the point where cars now whiz by nonstop just a few feet from the order window. Still, Kayuta stands proud and passive on the ever-encroaching roadside, a paean to the ice cream palaces of our youth. Always there, right up around the bend, giving a red-roofed wink to nostalgia, yet forging ahead with new additions and new ideas for generations of travelers to come.

There are hundreds of Kayutas all across Upstate New York. And I find that quite comforting.

During my travels around New York State, I have certainly had my share of ice cream cones. One in particular stands alone above the others. Donnelly's Ice Cream in Saranac Lake is perhaps the smallest walk-in stand in the state. You walk in on the right side of the building and are immediately met with the faces of the chirpy and friendly young servers behind the counter. You order and pick up at the same location and then exit out the door on the left, just five feet away. There really isn't much more room for anything else.

"It sure is small, no doubt about it," Peter Donnelly told me. "About thirteen by fifteen feet is all we got. But it is enough."

To get to know Pete Donnelly is to get a glimpse of the hardy and hearty folks that live in the High Peaks region of Upstate. I spent a couple of hours with him one August afternoon sitting on an old stone wall in front of the original Donnelly homestead. The view is breathtaking. The whole panorama of the Adirondacks sprawls out in front of you as if you can reach out and pluck a pine tree from old Mt. Pisgah.

"The whole ice cream thing started way back in 1953," Pete began in his straightforward, no-nonsense manner. "We always had a big dairy operation here for generations," he said as he swept his hand over the landscape, which includes several barns, farmhouses, and outbuildings. "I was ten years old when my two aunts, Rita Donnelly and Mary Sheehan, went to Atlantic City for a dairy show. While they were there they saw a new, odd contraption for making ice cream, and they just bought it. It was a 1953 Cherry-Burrell model, which was made over in Little Falls," he continued.

The machine was unique in its design because it featured only one flavor combination system a day. "We built the ice cream store in 1953. The women of the family always worked it down through the generations. Aunts, nieces, cousins, even my mother, Marion, always ran the place. I stayed in the back helping out and fixing things. But make no mistake about it. The women of the Donnelly clan ran this thing and still do. In fact my fourteen-year-old niece, Ellen, is inside working right now," he chuckled. "Fourth generation, yessir."

Donnelly's customers line up at the miniscule shop from the minute it opens until it closes. Like almost every other business in the North Country, it is a seasonal place.

"We like to say we are open from Memorial Day to Labor Day. But watch out if we get an early warm day," he said. "The phone will start ringing and people will stop by asking are we going to open? We tell them to hang on until Memorial Day. In fact, last year on Memorial Day it was cold and there was a big old snowcap up there on old Whiteface, but still they came for our ice cream," he declared as he pointed across the road to the nearly five-thousand-foot-tall Whiteface Mountain.

I asked Pete what sets his ice cream apart from the many hundreds of little stands like it. "I settle for nothing but the best. We may be small, but we are good. Our ice cream has the highest butter fat content you can get. We use only fresh fruits in our flavors. We even use real maple syrup in our maple cones. It's a good little spot," he said as he took off his Donnelly's Ice Cream ball cap and rubbed his forehead. "I will be honest with you. I never thought it would amount to what it is today. Grandparents bring their little grandkids in and tell them stories about stopping here forty or fifty years ago. It just makes you feel real good."

As the time approached for me to leave the stone wall and hit the road again, Pete looked up with his twinkly eyes and said, "How about taking a cone on the road with you, Chuck?"

He guided me inside the tiny stand past the line of customers, and he stepped back behind to the ice cream machine. "Here it is," he said patting the old grey metal unit.

"You mean that is the old 1953 Cherry-Burrell?" I asked.

"Take a look, I put that sign up years ago," he said as he pointed to a handwritten sign on the side of the machine. It read: "Donnelly's opened in 1953 . . . With the Same Machine!"

"Yup, same one. Still runs perfectly. They don't make them anymore so if something breaks down I just make the replacement parts myself." He then leaned over, grabbed a cone, and, with a flourish that belied his seventy years, Pete Donnelly made me one of the best-tasting ice cream cones I have ever had.

I really believe that. He, of course, already knew it.

31

FRIDAY FISH FRY

Rensselaer

$\mathcal{F}$ood traditions can start in the oddest of ways. Got one pig too many? Throw him in a fire pit and let's call it a pig roast. Do you have an abundance of corn? Call the neighbors and let's have a husking party. Got a cousin who knows how to make a delicious pancake batter? Open up the fire house door and let's have a pancake breakfast. Too many clams? It is clambake time! Got a gooey, sugary chunk of fluff that you don't know what to do with? Shove it on a stick and hold it over a fire and—voilà—a marshmallow roast! Have some leftover graham crackers and chocolate to go with it? Even better.

All kidding aside, it is easy to see how so many of our longstanding food traditions may have begun. From the puny harvests of the earliest Pilgrim days, when everybody shared everything, to modern day fundraisers, where "all-you-can-eats" bring whole communities together to share chicken and biscuits or spaghetti or flapjacks while contributing to a local charity, food has been the central gathering focus down through the years. It has created its own life force and has given us so many of our favorite customs and traditions.

But how about a food tradition that came from on high? Literally.

For ages the Vatican issued strict orders that Catholics were banned from eating meat on Fridays. When I was a kid in the 1950s, our Catechism class was taught that we were not to eat meat on Fridays because this was the day Christ was crucified, and giving up meat was our weekly sacrifice in his honor. We did this religiously (no pun intended).

We dreaded Fridays.

Mark and Priscilla Halsey take a fish fry break on the front lawn of their legendary eatery.

Mom would pack up the good old American cheese sandwich for us to take to school. No trading lunches on that day. Peanut butter and jelly was another good sandwich to pull off the bench, but we had plenty of that every day anyway. Tuna? Not if you are nine years old. A salad? Don't even go there.

Eventually this edict from Rome began to show fissures, and adherence to the meat ban was less strict. By the time the Second Vatican Council ended its controversial confab in 1965, the Catholic Church would be forever changed. Gone, or approaching the exit door, were the Latin mass, women wearing tissues on their head, and fasting during Lent. Marching in the new front door of the Catholic Church were folk masses, a larger role for women in the church, and sporty new outfits for the nuns.

Also, farewell Friday meat ban. We hardly knew ye.

But the one thing that did come out of the Catholic insistence of a meatless Friday was a better appreciation of fish. Kids in my generation never ate it, especially in Upstate New York, where we were as far from the rocky coast of Maine as you could get and still be in the same time zone. So fish needed to be, how shall we say, repurposed.

The number of Catholics in the fish audience Upstate is astounding. The Rochester diocese alone has 350,000 Catholics; in Buffalo that figure doubles. Fully a quarter of the population of Albany is Catholic. Even in Central New York the numbers are staggering. In Oneida County a whopping 35 percent of its citizens are Roman Catholics. So the lowly fish was ready for the big time. Especially on Fridays.

Although the custom of a Friday fish fry has been going on since, well, a piece of fish was first thrown in a fryer, the ones in Upstate take on a whole new meaning. Thank a large and aggressive Knights of Columbus organization within the church for that. During Lent, on Friday, on holidays, or just whenever they felt like it, it seems every Knights of Columbus group threw on a fish fry. They did it during the ban. They did it when the ban came with an "optional" box. And they still do it today. In many rural towns "K of C fish night" is an important time for socializing, for fundraising, for fellowship, and for a friendly meetup of the country and city mice.

Changes in the way we ate our fish were in the making well before the ban was lifted in 1966. Even McDonald's got in on the action. One of its hamburger franchisees in a heavily Catholic area insisted that a burger alternative would sell on Fridays. Ray Kroc, the owner of the company, gave the store manager a challenge: You come up with an idea, and I will too. The store manager, Lou Groen, came up with Filet-O-Fish. Kroc came up with the Hula Burger (grilled pineapple with cheese). In 1963, both were offered on two consecutive Fridays in Cleveland with the most popular choice destined to become a McDonald's staple. It is unknown how many Hula Burgers were sold that weekend, but an educated guess would be close to none. In contrast, millions of Filet-O-Fish sandwiches have been sold since then, on Fridays and every day.

I give mighty credit to the Knights of Columbus as well as the Golden Arches for bringing the eating of fish to the forefront in Upstate New York (and elsewhere) in the early 1960s. Soon fish was fun. Breaded and fried haddock and cod all of a sudden became "the next best thing." Fish was trendy. Fish was cool.

The fish fry soon became a type of standalone brick-and-mortar business where you could get your fish fix every day and all day long. And Upstate has some real winners!

Boice's Fish Fry in Fort Johnson offers a remarkable raw bar as well as a good old plank sandwich. Locals pack the place on weekends. It is actually located in a remote little map dot called Church Corners, just north of the New York State Thruway and just south of the Great Sacandaga Lake. A perfect place for a fish fry!

The Syracuse Suds Factory is a modern brew pub with a serious bar that is well stocked with their own homebrew, and a menu that includes a Brewmasters Chili, a Brewmasters Bratwurst, and beer-battered everything. They also have a popular, award-winning Friday night fish fry. When it opened in 1993, Syracuse Suds Factory became the first commercial brewery to open in the Salt City in more than three decades. Get there early for this one. Add a cup of their excellent New England clam chowder for the perfect end-of-the-week fish treat here in Syracuse.

A personal favorite fish repast is the giant ale-battered plank I get as often as I can at the Andes Hotel. While not a traditional fish fry place, it is a very good meal in a very historic setting. Every time I go, the ale-battered fish fillet gets bigger and bigger and tastier and tastier. It comes with fried-to-perfection chips (potato wedges) and a creamy, tangy tartar sauce. I swear the most recent time I ordered this the plate it was served on was invisible! The plank was that big. This historic hotel, built in 1850 and located high up in the Delaware County Catskills (hence the name Andes), offers a real slice of Americana with its long front porch overlooking the quiet main street, some lively entertainment out back in the thatched roof "Summershack," and some of the best fish and chips in Upstate.

Seafood lovers in the Hudson Valley swear by Joe Willy's Fish Shack on Old Route 9. It has a full menu of seafood delicacies and a fish fry that is talked about from Poughkeepsie to Catskill. Let me tell you two key components to the success of Joe Willy's fry: $10.99 and "all you can eat." Need I say more? It is also one of the only places I have heard of that features many gluten-free items on its seafood menu. Cozy dining room with a stark, bleached-white skeleton of a dead fish on the wall. Kind of ironic that the name of the town where Joe Willy's Fish Shack is located is Fishkill.

The Capital District is loaded with famous fish fry establishments. Bob and Ron's was located on Central Avenue when I went to college in Albany in 1967. It still is. In fact it has been there for more than sixty years. Perhaps the quintessential fish fry place, they sell thousands of fish fry sandwiches a year, and their huge sign with the red fishhook arrow pointing the way has been hooking customers for three generations, since long before the sprawling mall sprang up just down the road. On Fridays it is not uncommon to see customers backed up several blocks on busy Central Avenue waiting to pull in for dinner. If there were such a thing as a fish fry Hall of Fame, Bob and Ron's would have been inducted into the initial class!

Ted's Fish Fry, even older than Bob and Ron's, is still at its original location in Watervliet, just a couple of miles north of Albany. Customers have demanded more locations and you can now find Ted Deeb's delicious fish (and original Greek chili dogs) at several Capital District locations. Ted's is no less an Albany landmark than the RCA Nipper dog high atop the warehouse on Broadway.

For a popular piece of Upstate folklore, head out to Doug's Fish Fry in the Finger Lakes region. Located just two blocks from stunning Skaneateles Lake, it is everything you want in a small town fish fry. I love this place, and the fish fry sandwich (and everything else) here is memorable. You can find Doug's at several locations now, from other standalone restaurants to food festivals to the New York State Fair, but this Jordan Street place in Skaneateles is the one that put Doug Clark on the map.

Clark is a bit of a Skaneateles icon. A familiar site on the streets of town and on the lake (for years he could be seen powering his 1961 motor craft, the *Little Fry*, over the pristine blue waters), Clark created a bit of a national kerfuffle in 1999 when he said he would ban Bill and Hillary Clinton from eating at his place if they showed up during a five-day vacation in the Finger Lakes. The whole Monica Lewinsky thing, don't you know. The media built this up to a titanic showdown. The confrontation between the ex-president and his soon-to-be senator wife and the gruff fish fry guy with the blue cap cocked jauntily on his head never occurred. But hate mail did, and you can still see it today on the walls of his restaurant.

Doug's is classic fish fry all the way. Stand in line to order (no waitresses), plastic plates and plastic utensils, brown paper on the tables, orders hollered out for pickup, and no tipping allowed.

For me, though, the best fish fry in Upstate takes a little work to get to. I first found it in 1967 on my way to Vermont for a weekend vacation from college. It was located on a (then) dirt road seemingly in the middle of nowhere east of Albany. I remember pulling up to this eatery, which had just one order window. There was no grass around the small building. Only dirt. The fish fry was memorable to say the least. Nothing fancy, but oh so delicious.

I recently went looking for Gene's and found it still there, at the very same location in Rensselaer.

Gene's Fish Fry is a seasonal place. But even though it is only open from May 1 to Labor Day, it is always busy. "Yes, the customers really never stop from the minute we open until we close," Mark Halsey, the owner, told me. "You should come by here at lunchtime. You will see all types lined up for a fish sandwich. Bankers, students, bikers, dump truck drivers, moms with little kids, just all types."

Mark was born in the fish restaurant. Well, almost. "My dad, the original Gene, opened up the business on June 5, 1961. I was just an infant, so my parents put me in a playpen in a corner of the store to keep an eye on me. So you really could say I grew up here," he laughed. "And after all these years that tradition still carries on. After my dad retired from the business I bought it. Years ago, when my daughter Alexia was just five days old, we strapped her in a car seat and brought her to work with us. We placed the seat right on the freezer next to the order window so my wife, Priscilla, could keep a close eye on the baby. So I guess it was like father like daughter. We both grew up here!"

Gene's has a full menu of typical roadside food items, including burgers, French fries, and milk shakes. But it is the fried fish sandwich that has brought thousands of customers here since 1961. "Folks just love our fish. We get the haddock shipped in from Boston a couple of times a week so it is always fresh. We cook it to perfection and serve it with our own special homemade tartar sauce and, if you wish, a serving of our famous home-made coleslaw. Folks go crazy for it all."

Gene's has always been kind of rolling against the tide. There is no dining room, just a patio with several wooden picnic tables under an overhang. Parking is troublesome, and the neighborhood has crept in on Gene's since it first opened up.

"In the beginning there was just us," Mark told me. "Maybe just one or two other stores. The folks going east would come upon us and stop for a bite before heading up to Lake Burden or over to Vermont. Now the neighborhood sure has changed."

You have to keep your eyes open when you are traveling the old Troy Road. You'll whiz by shopping malls, medical plazas, housing developments, and other hallmarks of suburbia. And then, appearing before you like a postcard from home, up pops the simple, low-slung white building with the fish sign on top of it. You will probably miss the turn into Gene's the first time you try (I have yet to perfect it), but like they always say, the catch is worth the chase.

Across the street is another venerable fish restaurant, Off-Shore Pier. It is a year-round seafood restaurant with a full sit-down dining room. It opened in 1976. "We've been friendly neighbors for more than thirty-five years," Mark Halsey told me. "We are very different. They are open twelve months of the year and offer many menu selections. Even though they are directly across the street from us, I don't even like to call them competitors. We are friends." It is hard to imagine that in a remote corner of the Capital District there is almost one hundred years of fish fry history on opposite sides of the road.

The fish fry served up at Mark and Priscilla's place is about the best you will find. On opening day in 1961, a fish fry at Gene's was a bargain at twenty-five cents. More than five decades later it is still a bargain at under five dollars. "We still have customers who were coming in here fifty years ago. We had a couple of customers who were married for sixty-five years. They came in here several times a week ever since we first opened up. We'd see them pull up and go ahead and fix their order: two fish frys, one order of French fries and two sodas. The same thing every time for fifty years. They met during World War II. A sweet, loving couple. The wife just passed away a couple of months ago. Now the gentleman comes in with his daughter. Some traditions are just hard to break I guess," Mark said softly.

There are several other great fish fry places in the Capital District, where more than a third of a million residents identify themselves as Catholics. So try them all. But if you are looking for Gene's, remember to keep your eyes open. If you are new to the area, it can be hard to find, but once you've found it you will definitely want to come back for more.

I know I did. It may have taken me since 1967 to do so, but I *did* come back!

32

BAKERIES
Boiceville

*B*akeries are nothing specific to the Upstate region. In every corner of America, from the glitziest main thoroughfare in Manhattan to the quietest dusty back roads of rural Pennsylvania and Kansas, you'll find good, down home bakeries. It seems to be something that America does and does well.

The thing that always gets me is the wide variety of specialties you can find in a bakery. Macaroon cookies, for example. To me, a macaroon was something any kid avoided like the plague. I mean, what are they anyways? Kind of cakey. Kind of almondy. Kind of ugly.

However, when I visited my daughter in Los Angeles recently she couldn't wait to take me to downtown LA to the newest macaroon bakery in town. The newest? You mean there is more than one?

Frances and I parked the car near the Biltmore Hotel on Grand Street and walked just a couple of blocks before I saw it. Huge floor-to-ceiling plate glass windows. Inside were shiny, gleaming tables holding dramatically backlit towers, no, *pyramids* of macaroons. The name of the patisserie is Bottega Louie. It was packed. The waiting line for macaroons snaked across the elegant dining room. Well-turned-out customers were ordering boxes and boxes of the round little cookies to go. The macaroons were every color imaginable, displayed in a pulsating pageant of pastry: Irish greens, blushing pastel pinks, sparkling whites, bright sunshiny yellows, and silvery grays. They were gorgeous.

Gee, I never had one of these things stuffed into my Roy Rogers lunch box when I went to school!

Sharon Burns-Leader and Nels Leader stand in front of Bread Alone's custom-made French oven.

Bakeries become touchstones to our past. When I was a kid in rural Upstate during the 1950s, I remember my cousins coming up from Brooklyn to visit us in the summer. One of the first things they unpacked was boxes of baked goods from their favorite bakery back in New York. Donuts, coffee cakes, cookies of all kinds and all of them boxed in a distinct blue-and-white carton. I'll never forget the elegant name inscribed across the front of the box: *Entenmann's*. Yes, they couldn't even venture across the George Washington Bridge for a weekend without their dearly beloved baked goods from home to accompany them. Now, that is product loyalty!

When I was a college student in 1968, I worked at night at Freihofer's Bakery in Albany. It was the premier, iconic Capital District bakery of its time (they are still in business). The factory was a big, rusty monster of a building tucked up in the Arbor Hill district. My friend from Sidney, Steve, and I would get out of class and go and check in for duty. We were just teenagers. Our fellow bakery workers were tough, seasoned, decades-long union workers. The women were tougher than the men. In fact, our supervisor was a woman. If you messed up, you could expect

Doris to come thundering down the line to you, starched white lab coat on, cat's-eye glasses swinging wildly from a gold chain around her neck. She'd get in your face, jab a red-lacquered fingertip in your chest and shout, "*Danish!*"

This was about as severe punishment as you could get at Freihofer's. Just shy of the dreaded Louisiana ring room but not quite the as bad as the feared batter room. Danish was a tough stint to pull because of the gooey mush that ultimately would cake your hands so thick that by the time you punched out, your fingers were literally welded together by a cement-like sugary coating. And the batter room, sort of a bakery gulag, was always a mess, always impossible to keep clean and always a hundred degrees.

My job was putting cherries on cupcakes. I stood at a conveyor line that dropped hundreds of cupcakes down in front of me. Ladies on either side would frost them in an instant, and then I would adeptly drop a half maraschino cherry smack dab in the middle of the creamy peak. Just writing this makes me sweat and also makes me think of the *I Love Lucy* scene where Lucy and Ethel were doing the same thing I did in 1968 in Albany. I can almost hear somebody yell, "Speed it up!"

So I know a little bit about bakeries. Very little.

It is true Americans are suckers for the sweet stuff. In Upstate there is no shortage of bake shops or bakeries of every stripe. Maybe over a thousand of them? Two thousand? Nobody has ever counted. One interesting quirk about a bake shop is the downright loyalty of its customers. Find a bakery that serves a good French baguette and you will go there for life. Know a place that makes the best chocolate chip cookie? You will tell your grandchildren about it. Or better yet you will take them there. Are you addicted to a neighborhood bake shop that makes a delicious almond torte? A good sign that you are in over your head is if you find yourself asking if they need part-time help at that bakery. And you don't even need a second job. Red flag! Bakeries are like that.

I have a friend who is a serious foodie through and through. He knows what he likes and will go to the ends of the earth to get it. I have seen him do it. With a bakery. We were driving through Albany one day and his eyes started to glaze over. I asked Dan if he was OK, and he told me about a bake shop he remembered in the area from years before. Like a bloodhound sniffing for the final clue, he followed his nose and his memory and we ended up at the wonderful Bella Napoli Bakery in Latham, New York.

My friend floated above the ground as he entered the bakery with us in tow. And he was right on the mark. This unforgettable place offers some of the most beautiful and delicious Italian (and other) sweet treats you will ever find. And it is very busy (it is one of those "take-a-number" places). Also, you know you are at the real deal when the counter clerk unspools a long piece of twine to wrap up your take-out box. That is a classic Old World touch. I loved this place.

It would take another whole book to list all of my favorite bakeries around the state. One good sign that a place is beloved by its customers is to see how old it is. Upstate has some real old timers! Wolter's Bakery opened in 1957 in Amherst and is still the place to go for apple strudels and holiday fruit cakes. In my hometown Foti's Bakery has been delivering homemade Italian loaves to Oneonta businesses and homes for more than a century. Perreca's in Schenectady's Little Italy has been using the same coal-fired oven to make their bread since 1913. Some people swear the raisin pumpernickel bread at Cohen's Bakery in Ellenville skips all mortals' hands and is delivered straight to the shelves of this one-hundred-year-old bakery by angels from heaven. Caffè Aurora in Poughkeepsie was famous for its petit fours when it opened back in 1941. First Lady Eleanor Roosevelt used to drive down from Hyde Park in her limousine to get a box for her husband, the president. The bakery is still famous for these delectable "small ovens."

And who knows how many of baseball's legendary Hall of Famers celebrated their big day in Cooperstown by walking the two blocks to Schneider's Bakery for a brownie or a special piece of cake. The bakery opened more than a half century *before* the Baseball Hall of Fame first opened its doors in 1939. I'll bet the Babe would have loved Schneider's.

It is hard not to get caught up in the latest bakery frenzy. New Yorkers line up at sunrise to get a coveted "cronut" in Manhattan. These croissant/donut hybrids are the new Krispy Kreme, which was the new Famous Amos, which was the new Twinkie. I mean, you just *had to* have one of these hot new items. After a while the cronut places will disappear just like

Krispy Kreme stock prices did about a decade ago, and folks will return to their old favorite corner bake shop.

But I would suggest to these wide-eyed lemmings waiting to fall off the next pastry cliff that age and patience has its rewards, too. Everything doesn't have to be the next hot new thing to be memorable. Sometimes it pays to go out of your way to a consistent, steady old friend. Take Deising's Bakery in Kingston for example. They have made more than seven million loaves of bread since Uwe Deising came to the United States after being named the "youngest master baker in Germany." They have only used two ovens since they opened their doors more than a half century ago. Cakes, pies, tortes, cookies, and homemade breads are their specialties. Consistent. Steady. Reliable. Patient. Beloved. An old friend. Now that is what makes a bakery.

And not a cronut to be found!

While driving through the Catskill Mountains recently my stomach told me it was snack time. Not quite dinner time, but definitely snack time. I was heading north on Route 28 from Kingston to Oneonta. I passed many quaint little towns along the way but nothing "poked" me to stop. The region is filled with history, and you pass through many of the ghost towns that are identified by sign only since they were erased through a rural version of urban removal. Call it rural removal.

In the early 1900s, the city of New York was growing fast and getting thirsty. They turned their parched eyes northward to the gleaming, pristine Catskill Mountains with their unlimited forests and waterways. For a half century, the engineers and city planners from downstate came to the mountains and finagled the property away from its owners through direct payment or eminent domain. With a massive stamp of government approval, monstrous dams were constructed in the region, stopping up small rivers and streams to create wide expanses of water called reservoirs. These would become the fountain from which Gothamites would drink.

These massive construction projects sank a number of little out-of-the-way towns and villages that simply could not withstand the force of a determined and very thirsty New York City. Some homes and businesses were moved. Literally dragged to other locations. Others were bulldozed to the ground. Cemeteries were dug up, and the dead of several generations were moved from their restful slumber. Churches, schools, homes, businesses, and more. Gone. Life changed for everyone in these Catskill valleys when the bulldozers and earth movers moved in during that time. Parts of towns that were once over there are now over here. Hamlets vanished. Places like Arena, Rock Royal, Cannonsville, Olive, West Hurley, Ashton, Glenford, Union Grove, Beerston, Rock Rift, and Bishop's Falls. All mixed up. All gone forever. Thousands of people were uprooted by a rural diaspora of tragic proportions.

I was driving this day over the road that traverses the Ashokan Reservoir, one of the more than a dozen manmade lakes that provides much of the water source for New York City, and the first one built in the Catskills. The Ashokan alone holds more than one hundred billion gallons of water. The strains of Jay Ungar and Molly Mason's haunting "Ashokan Farewell" can be imagined lilting over the gigantic water creation, which suffocated the little towns whose memories rest on the silty bottom of the basin.

As I headed northward through the reservoir area, I came upon a sign for the tiny hamlet of Boiceville. Part of it was moved from its original place. There is a bar, a school that serves the whole area, a business that stitches the white stars for most of our American flags, some eateries, and a few tidy homes. My stomach was still purring as I glanced around for a place to stop for a bite. Any place. And then I saw it.

"Bread Alone Bakery: Made by Hand Each and Every Day," the sign said. It was in an odd place that required me to do a quick U-turn just to get into the parking lot. There were a couple of cars in the lot, so I thought this might be as good a place as any to appease my hunger. And was it ever. Little did I know I had just discovered the best bakery in Upstate New York.

The first thing you are assaulted with when you step into the small bakery showroom is the delightful aroma of bread baking. It is a sensory trigger that immediately takes you back to your youth and your Mom or Grandma making rolls or biscuits for the Sunday dinner. The bakery is quite small so you look for the end of the line and slowly shuffle along past the bread and pastry cases up to the order counter.

The bread showcases here are among the most awesome I have ever seen. Huge loaves of various breads are piled atop one another in a display of natural beauty and grandeur that is hard to overstate. Massive loaves, like cords of wood, are stacked up together: multigrain, organic raisin nut, sesame, onion and olive focaccia, French sourdough, and their famous peasant bread. The variety seems endless.

"Our concept is back to the land," said Nels Leader, vice president and chief operating officer of Bread Alone. "Our bread is all handmade, baked fresh everyday using only the best, most wholesome wheat, flour and ingredients. Everything is top shelf here. We use dairy products from Kingston, eggs from a nearby farm, butter from Vermont, and our flour comes from one of the best flour mills in Canada. My dad, Dan, was one of the first to use the 'back to the land' concept. He was a graduate of the Culinary Institute of America and had a high regard for quality foods. He insisted that we know where every ingredient came from. Not just from some wholesaler someplace. In fact, he once went to North Dakota just to inspect the actual wheat field that we were getting our grain from back then."

"Yes, Dan was a true pioneer," Sharon Burns-Leader said. She is Dan's partner and is co-owner of Bread Alone. "A pioneer in the sense that he had a dream to open a European-inspired artisan bread bakery back in the time of Wonder Bread. I was lucky enough to come along and help Dan realize that dream."

A key part of any successful bakery is the oven, and Bread Alone has a humdinger!

"More than a quarter century ago Dan hired one of the most renowned, third-generation oven masters from France, Andre LeFort, to come to Boiceville and custom make our brick bread ovens."

They are works of art. Gigantic brick walls with silvery doors. The bricks are aged and seasoned with the aroma of tens of thousands of loaves baked in them since the oven was created more than thirty years ago.

"Here is the man's signature plaque," Sharon said as she pointed to a blackened iron plate on the ovens. It read: Made by LeFort. "It is ironic that LeFort is French for 'the oven,'" she laughed.

I peered inside the massive ovens and observed row after endless row of giant loaves of bread basking in the warmth of the old, custom, wood-fired oven. The work area is stacked with towering racks of bread, ready to be presented out front or shipped out.

"Over time our success made it possible for us to open two other Bread Alone locations. They are more typical of a café or a small restaurant than our Boiceville shop. Each of the other two, in Rhinebeck and Woodstock, has full menus including breakfasts and lunches, and lots of hot items like sandwiches, quiches, soups and specialty burgers. They are very popular, but we still make all the bread right here in these old ovens in Boiceville," Nels told me.

This little bakery in the middle of nowhere stands out head and shoulders above the other bakeries that I have been to. Of course, "best bakery" is all in one's mind. Everybody has a favorite, and I realize that. For my cousins from Brooklyn back in the 1950s it was Entenmann's. To Eleanor Roosevelt it was Caffè Aurora in Poughkeepsie.

But I can promise you this. If you stop by this Boiceville bakery and order one of their raspberry tarts, your mouth will start watering long before you even maneuver the marble sized raspberries off the top of the pastry and into your mouth. I can also guarantee that if you order two or more loaves of any of their home baked breads, you will definitely need both hands to carry them out to your car. And if you ever should dare to purchase a Morning Glory Muffin, filled with carrots, pecans, apples, cinnamon and coconut, you will find yourself never wanting to share this little secret place with even your best friend. You will want to keep it all to yourself!

Dan Leader once dreamed that "if you bake it they will come," whether in Manhattan or Quebec or the Catskills. His goal was to provide his loyal customers with something that was beautiful, timeless, and wholesome. Bread Alone in tiny Boiceville, New York, is the bakery of your dreams. Take my word for it.

33

BUCKWHEAT PANCAKES

Penn Yan

*A*sk somebody what the definition of a pancake is and you will get pretty much the same answer every time.

Then ask that same person what a johnnycake is? Or a hoe-cake? Or a flapjack? Or a silver dollar cake? Well, they are all pretty much the same thing with slight variations. Johnnycakes find their foundation in gruel. Hoecakes were breakfast flatbreads cooked on the flat end of a heated hoe by slaves and farm workers in the early 1800s in the South. Silver dollar cakes were simply smaller pancakes, about the size of an old large silver dollar. Whatever you call them, these fluffy batter creations have been around almost since recorded time itself.

In fact the word *pancake* first appeared in the English form in the early 1400s. Generally, the origins of pancakes trace back to ancient Greece. Upstate New York, while holding no proprietary claim on pancakes, can trace their production back through a couple of different centuries at a minimum.

A perfect way to gauge this lineage is through the historic and magnificent old mills that sprouted up across Upstate. Take the New Hope Mills, for example, in Auburn. They have been churning out pancake mixes since 1823 and are today one of the oldest mills in the nation. Their product is still popular with adults and children alike, and their old mill and retail store is a fun place to visit, experience history, and enjoy some wonderful tasty treats. The original recipe for New Hope Mills banana caramel pancake mix produces one of the best tasting morning eye openers you will ever have.

The giant griddle used to make the world's largest pancake hangs on the exterior of Birkett Mills. (Photo courtesy of www.thebirkettmills.com)

The café at New Hope Mills is a popular gathering spot for locals, especially on Saturday mornings. That is when they have a Paul Bunyon–esque offering that is hard to resist: all-you-can-eat New Hope Mills pancakes for under five dollars. By the way, the current record for one seating is twenty-two and a half pancakes!

There is much history in our area regarding old grist, wheat, flour, grain, and paper mills. Not many of them continue to make products. Still fewer are even in working condition. Several water mills continue to be open across Upstate, allowing visitors to see these old wonders still in action. Some of the best are Hanford Mills in East Meredith, Dard Hunter's Paper Mill in Marlboro, and Cavern Creek Grist Mill in Howes Cave.

Still the history of mills and pancake mixes is in our region's DNA.

"Bainbridge might be small, but we can actually claim to be the home of America's first instant breakfast," Mary Drachler, president of the Bainbridge Museum, told me. "A mill was established in Smithville Flats in 1832 and was owned for decades by a Civil War veteran named Captain

Uriah Rorapaugh. He sold it to Frederick Hansmann in 1905, and he went into the pancake and flour business. In the early part of the twentieth century Mr. Hansmann came up with a startling new innovation," Drachler said. "A pancake mix that was instant, all you needed was water. No eggs, flour, mixing, or measuring. Just pour it in the bowl, add a cup of water, and you were all set to eat! Of course, it was revolutionary to the way Americans dined for breakfast, and it made Mr. Hansmann a very wealthy man."

Although Hansmann family members still reside in the Smithville Flats area, no mill exists for history lovers to go and explore the Birthplace of the American Instant Breakfast.

"After Mr. Hansmann died the family kept the business up, and it was eventually bought and moved to Bainbridge. It was here for years, and many local folks worked at the mill making the pancake mix. Unfortunately, the company moved to Binghamton in 1995, and about ten years later it was destroyed by a flood. The business never reopened."

America's first instant breakfast, a just-add-water pancake mix, done in by water.

For an old, historic mill that continues churning out a legacy products today, I would have to point you to a hulking yet somewhat graceful two-hundred-year-old structure that straddles a water outlet running between two of Upstate's Finger Lakes, Keuka and Seneca Lakes.

"Yes, this old mill was built on the water here in Penn Yan around 1797," Jeff Gifford, president and owner of Birkett Mills told me. "In fact, even though the mill has expanded greatly over the centuries, there are actually places at Birkett Mills where the water still runs underneath the building."

While this chapter is about the long history of pancakes in our region, pancake mixes are no longer the leading product to come out of Birkett. "It used to be, a long time ago," Gifford said. "But now we have other products that are bigger sellers. But we like the little niche that we have. Birkett Mills is the largest manufacturer of buckwheat products in the world. And that includes our buckwheat pancake mix."

I was almost too embarrassed to ask. "What is buckwheat anyway?"

"A lot of people ask that," he said. "Buckwheat is not related to wheat. It is a grain that has considerable healthy attributes to it. Ironically, those same attributes make it a difficult crop to grow. Buckwheat won't take to pesticides, so you'll find it mostly as a marginal crop rather than a main one. Where an average farmer's yield can be around sixty bushels of wheat an acre, you'll be glad to get between twenty and twenty-five bushels of buckwheat from that same acre.

"But you can still find plenty of it throughout the western New York region, especially around Monroe County. In fact I once harvested buckwheat on a dairy farm to work my way through the State University of New York at Brockport. Little did I imagine that one day I would own a prestigious buckwheat mill," he smiled.

Birkett Mills has been a sturdy and reliable friend to its host community since long before Jeff Gifford came along. "Our buckwheat pancake mix really made us famous. It makes a different, heartier and darker type of pancake. People love them and many area restaurants serve our brand. Many other brand name buckwheat products that you find on national supermarket shelves use us as their source. We get our buckwheat from local producers by tractor trailer delivery, and still other out-of-state growers send us their buckwheat supply by train. We only have about thirty employees so it sure keeps us all busy."

Today, the top product sold by Birkett Mills is pastry flour. They have a couple of popular buckwheat products, too. Pocono kasha is a roasted buckwheat cereal. Another is Wolff's organic buckwheat groats. Both are kosher items and are sold all over the world.

"Our fastest growing product right now is the naturally gluten-free Pocono Cream of Buckwheat cereal. It has really taken off over the last several years," Gifford said.

Although the buckwheat pancake mix is made on a smaller level than it used to be, there is still a reminder of something big at Birkett Mills. I mean really big.

"You must be talking about the griddle outside," Gifford said.

You can't miss it. There, hanging on the side of the mill is the largest pancake griddle you will ever see. It harkens back to a fun and festive tradition at Birkett Mills.

"Yes, we used to host the Penn Yan Buckwheat Festival. We held it for several years until it got so big we simply couldn't do it any longer. But it was great fun. It was a whole community-wide event. Everybody of all ages got involved. People ate buckwheat bread and rolls, buckwheat pizza, and even buckwheat ice cream. Entertainers like Charlie Daniels, Chubby Checker, and Lee Greenwood came to perform for the big crowds.

"One year we decided that we were going to make the largest pancake in the world. Well, before long this dream started to become a reality. An enormous two-piece griddle was built. A bunch of volunteers stacked up wood for the fire. We made up some buckwheat pancake batter and mixed it in a brand new cement truck. And then with the whole town looking on we poured it out of the truck and onto the griddle.

"What a time it was. The fire was roaring and everybody was having a grand old time. At just the right moment a crane moved into position and flipped the giant pancake. And when it was cooked just right a local church sold pieces of it to the townsfolk. A dairy over in Batavia brought down a huge pat of butter. Some of our maple producers brought over real maple syrup in big five-gallon cans to pour on top. And yes, the *Guinness Book of World Records* people certified it as the largest pancake ever made. Almost thirty feet in diameter. And the original griddle is still hanging from the side of the building," he said.

More than a quarter of a century later, times have changed in Penn Yan and at the mill. "We just couldn't hold the festival any more. When we started out doing it we used to close down for as long as three weeks just to prepare for it. Now we run our operation twenty four hours a day. But it sure was fun while it lasted."

There is much more to Birkett Mills than meets the eye. This old place, squashed between two Finger Lakes, has a bloodline that runs deep and true throughout the region.

"This mill is a lot more than boards and rooms and machinery. This place is all about the people. Every day when I come to work I try to remind myself about those that came before me. For two centuries people have been coming into this mill, sometimes into the same rooms and sometimes even using the *same equipment* that we have today. There is a rich history here, and it lies with the people. For ten generations people have been making a quality product right here. These people are real to me, both those in the present and those in the past.

"Every year we hold a big Christmas party for all of our workers' kids. Each child gets a gift specific to their wishes. It is really a warm and festive time. And every summer we hold a big employees picnic. All our workers enjoy a big day of food and friendship. Many of our former employees come back to reminisce about the old days. Widows stop by and tell the stories of their husbands' time at the mill. It is important to me that these people really do want to come back and share a story or just say hello. And we have plenty of hamburgers and hot dogs and barbecue chicken for all the families to enjoy."

"No buckwheat pancakes?" I asked.

"No, not on that day," the owner smiled.

34

COOKBOOKS

Sharon Springs

*R*egional cookbooks come in all shapes and forms. For me, the best ones
are the small, sometimes hand-stapled recipe books that churches, organi-
zations, and schools put out as fundraisers. There are thousands of them.
These are the bibles of small town cooking. If you were ever going to find
out what goes into Cousin Emma's apple tart pie filling, no doubt the
secret will be in her church cookbook. If you want to know exactly how
Ruby Johnson gets her ears of corn to come out perfect *every single time*,
chances are Miss Ruby spilled the beans in the neighborhood fundraising cooking pamphlet. And how do the Wilson women keep producing
county fair winning pickled vegetables year after year after year? I'll bet
you can find the answer in one of the hundreds of 4-H community recipe
books that are in print from coast to coast.

Ask Grandma what the hand-me-down recipe for her fruit bread is
and she'll probably tell you it's none of your business and then shoo you
from her kitchen. But give Grandma the opportunity to brag about that
same recipe in a church cookbook and she'll jump at the chance. Nothing
like a little friendly competition to squeeze out one's closely held family
recipes. I mean, even Grandma likes to show off once in a while.

And that it why I love these little cookbooks. They are where the
grandmothers of America spill their delicious secrets.

Agreeing to the fact that these are the best sources for wonderful
recipes, let's set them aside and take a look at a few really great, widely
respected cookbooks that spring from the kitchens of Upstate New York.

Josh Kilmer-Purcell (left) and Brent Ridge are known for their many television appearances. You can usually get them to autograph a cookbook for you at their shop in Sharon Springs.

The Moosewood Restaurant is a good place to start. This legendary Ithaca restaurant has been located in the same spot, a renovated city school building, for more than four decades. The Moosewood Collective is a unique collaboration of fourteen women and five men who come from different backgrounds, but whose unifying force is to provide good, healthy, and creative foods to their customers. Each member of the collective, including musicians, chefs, artists, teachers, trainers, actors, journalists, and others, contributes to the whole that is Moosewood. The menu at the restaurant is eclectic and ever changing. It is one of the most popular restaurants in this college city in the Finger Lakes region, and reservations are strongly suggested.

The Moosewood Collective also produces cookbooks. With more than a dozen in print, including their 2013 *Moosewood Restaurant Favorites* edition, Moosewood is now nationally recognized as one of the leading restaurants in all of New York State. Their cookbooks have sold over a million copies and have won several James Beard awards. Although comprehensive in scope, the *Favorites* cookbook is nothing fancy. The chapters read like a primer to all-American eats: dips and spreads, sandwiches, casseroles, stews, burgers, strudels, salads, and desserts are the topics of just a few.

Despite the chamber of commerce–inspired title, the *I Love New York Cookbook* comes with some pretty impressive pedigrees. Chef Daniel Humm and general manager Will Guidara were the culinary magicians who transformed New York City's Eleven Madison Park restaurant from a French brasserie into perhaps the quintessential Empire State gastronomical showcase (and garnering it a four-star *New York Times* review along the way.).

The duo traveled to hundreds of area food destinations and interviewed countless providers to come up with a hefty work of good, old-fashioned New York food attitude. They even visited more than thirty local farms to research their products and puzzle together their recipes. The stories in their book are excellent, but don't think this is a light read by any means. Clocking in at well over five hundred pages, this is heavy lifting for the serious foodie. The book has a focus on the Big Apple, but those throughout the Upstate region will enjoy the narrative of this great New York food book.

After all, we are the ones who grow the stuff!

Next up we meet Aunt Sally.

If you can get your hands on *Aunt Sally's Adirondack Kitchen Cookbook*, you will be holding a popular journal of legendary Upstate food lore. Aunt Sally (Sally Longo) is a popular journalist, cooking instructor, and food writer who has combed those little hand-stapled recipe books (spoken of at the beginning of this chapter) and interviewed cooks from all over the Adirondack region to come up with one of the most popular books of its type.

Sally Longo is also a well-known caterer who has spent more than two decades preparing everything in her book, including pumpkin walnut bread, Gail's Buckeye Balls, Not-Flat Chocolate Chip Cookies, Grandma Dott's Red Cabbage, smashed cauliflower, and her own famous Mushroom Knapsacks for her extensive rolodex of satisfied customers.

Although Sally's homespun book (with gorgeous North Country photographs by Gerry Lemmo) was printed in 2007, it is still a big seller. Her specialty is "plan ahead meals," and if you are heading out for a week in the Adirondacks with your family, this cookbook is as necessary as a can of black fly repellant.

And now for a little pizzazz.

Josh Kilmer-Purcell and Dr. Brent Ridge bring a dash of Hollywood to the small town of Sharon Springs. The two, known as the Fabulous Beekman Boys, settled in this Upstate map dot in 2007. They bought one of the region's great old nineteenth-century mansions, the Beekman Farm, and moved in—muck boots, goats, Farmer John, filming crew and all!

Farmer John Hall oversaw the operation while Josh and Brent, who were married there in 2013, starred in the reality show *The Fabulous Beekman Boys*. The show was originally aired on the Planet Green network and ultimately on the Cooking Channel. They opened up a high-end mercantile on the two-block Main Street of Sharon Springs called Beekman 1802. In 2012, the pair entered the twenty-first season of the hit competition show *The Amazing Race*. And amazing it was.

They won. *A million bucks!*

"That show really put us over the top," Josh told me. "Our legions of fans were cheering us along the whole way. I think we even surprised ourselves by winning the thing," he laughed. The million-dollar prize allowed the pair to pay off the mortgage on their farm and live permanently in the village. Before becoming a real life *Green Acres* couple, Josh was a *New York Times* best-selling author and Brent was a New York City physician and an associate of Martha Stewart.

Josh and Brent are true believers in using local products in their endeavors, both food and otherwise, and they are among the greatest supporters of Upstate New York. They host festivals in Sharon Springs that bring thousands of visitors (along with their dollars) to the bucolic Schoharie Valley each year. And you never know when one of their celebrity friends will show up. Martha Stewart? Rosie O'Donnell? Sitcom stars? Yes, they have all GPS'd Sharon Springs and attended one of the Beekman Boys' celebrations.

"We started putting together a cookbook a few years ago," Brent said. "It just seemed like a natural extension to all that we do at the farm and in town. We both know the value of good, homegrown food. We are both from rural areas and when we lived in New York City we even had a roof-top garden on our building. We called our first cookbook the *Beekman 1802 Heirloom Cookbook*. It is filled with recipes that mean so much to Josh and me. Family recipes. Local recipes from our friends and neighbors. All using simple products found in our gardens and at the farm stands throughout the area. The book is divided by seasons. We did our first cookbook because we noticed that the food section of our website was the most visited section. Needless to say, our first cookbook was a huge success."

The *Beekman 1802 Heirloom Cookbook* cued up a demand for an encore. "Our next book is a dessert cookbook," Josh said. "It is filled with great family recipes and stories. It really is the stories that grab people's attention. And we want these cookbooks to really, truly become family heirlooms. Like in the old days. Something to be handed down from generation to generation. And I think it is this old-fashioned approach to a cookbook that really resonates with shoppers. We appeared on QVC with our book and sold eight thousand copies in five minutes."

Each of the cookbooks has pouches, blank pages, and areas for the book's owners to make notes, jot down memories, or share their own thoughts to be handed down. The photographs are stunning, many of the stories are touching and the recipes are tantalizing.

"My favorite is my Aunt Hazel's Oatmeal Cream Pie Cookie. She made them when I was a kid and I still make them up here at our Upstate farm. They are filled with a ginger cream and are just so sentimental to me. The funny thing is, Chuck, a lot of people ask us if these really are old family favorites or did we just make that up? Well, yes, they are heirloom recipes from the many generations of cooks in both of our families. In fact, when we did a thirty-nine-city book tour for the *Beekman 1802 Heirloom Dessert Cookbook* last year, we had a stop in North Carolina. We looked down the line and who was standing there but dear Aunt Hazel with a tray of her famous cookies. We passed them out to our fans," Brent laughed.

A third cookbook has just hit the bookstores. The *Beekman 1802 Heirloom Vegetable Cookbook* is loaded with more than one hundred farm-tested recipes. "We have partnered with D. Landreth Seed Company in this book. They are the oldest seed company in America. They've been so helpful to us. And the book is gorgeous with lots of old drawings from old seed catalogs throughout the covers," Brent told me.

From QVC to Hollywood to *The Amazing Race* to the Cooking Channel to Martha Stewart and beyond, it has been a heady couple of years for these two engaging young men. "It has been fun going all around the world and being on TV and everything," Josh said. "But our hearts are right here in Upstate New York, in this beautiful Schoharie Valley that we love. We hope everybody will come up to little Sharon Springs sometime and say hello."

35

DINERS
Unadilla

I love a diner.

I am a big guy, but no matter how small the little train car-sized eatery is, I will try and squeeze my mighty girth into the red leather booth (which is usually ripped), open up the plastic covered menu (which usually has the parting remnants of the previous person's just-eaten meal on it), and sentimentally eye the little flip jukebox hanging from the wall over the table (most often it does not work). None of this matters.

Like I said. I love a diner.

With the hallmark of round leatherette counter stools, cheap-but-hearty breakfasts, and lots and lots of stainless steel, diners have been around for 150 years. They dot the landscape of New England and Upstate New York perhaps more than any other region in the country. The first diners were found in Rhode Island and Massachusetts, and soon the concept spread across the country. Operating a diner was an "easy in" for small entrepreneurs with little start-up money. This fit the burgeoning immigrant profile perfectly. It is estimated that as many as six hundred diners were started by Greek immigrants in New York City alone during the 1950s.

Diners are as much a part of the American landscape as a motel with one neon letter out in its Open sign. Or the service station with just two pumps and a Coca Cola chest cooler. Or even a roadside anomaly like a tepee selling Indian crafts or a petrified creatures playland featuring the prehistoric finds from the muck of a hundred centuries ago. Actually, you will find these last two along Route 20, the pre-Thruway ribbon of

181

Howdy, folks! This diner had a long, long journey to its destination in Upstate. It traveled thousands of miles over several decades before finally opening near Duanesburg.

highway that bisects the state. Petrified Creatures Museum, in Richfield Springs, has been intriguing adults and trying to scare children since the 1940s. And the Te-Pee (yes it is built like a Native American tent home) has been selling Indian drums and moccasins since it opened in Cherry Valley in 1950.

Both are on the longest surface road in the state. To find some great diners, one only has to stay on this legendary highway for an hour or two either way.

The Quack Diner in Madison opened its doors in 1947. Over time, it has been fancied up to become a comfortable, attractive full service family restaurant. It is now called Quack's Village Inn. Everybody still calls it a diner. It is a real beacon of nostalgia in this rural central part of the state. It is impossible to get a bad meal at Quack's. They specialize in homemade rolls (try the made from scratch onion rolls) and hearty breakfasts. Be careful in August, however. Tens of thousands of visitors descend on Madison and its neighboring town of Bouckville for the largest open-air antique show in the East. The event is usually the third weekend in August, and Quack's Diner, I mean, um, Quack's *Village Inn* becomes the busiest place along the highway.

An interesting piece of diner eye candy can be found on Route 20 in Princetown near Rotterdam. The New Chuck Wagon Diner looks like it just came off a Hollywood stage set. It is small, chrome, rounded, covered with neon, and serves delicious meals. But the real bee's knees here is the sign. It is an original blinking neon sign with a cowboy on it flashing "Howdy Y'all." It is beautiful, and its story is fascinating.

The whole diner is 1950s original right down to the music blaring out of the little individual booth jukeboxes (yes, they work). The diner began its peripatetic wanderings toward Upstate in 1956 in Singac, New Jersey, where it was built. From there, it moved to Champaign, Illinois, where the cowboy waved at travelers to stop in for some then-new Kentucky Fried Chicken. The Chuck Wagon Diner was only the fourteenth KFC franchise in America. It later changed its name to the Elite Diner and meandered to Michigan where it was eventually abandoned. The present owners, Tom and Sally Ketchum, rescued it from oblivion and brought it piece by piece to its present location. There was cause for great satisfaction when the final piece to this nostalgic puzzle was found in Illinois: the magnificent original blinking cowboy sign.

There is probably nothing wrong with going to, say, a Johnny Rockets franchise to sample some faux-1950s good times and good food. But for the real deal you should come and bring your family to the New Chuck Wagon Diner in Princetown.

A couple of hours west of the New Chuck Wagon Diner, but on the same highway, is a diner that will cause you to stop and take a second look. It is Hunter's Dinerant in Auburn. I guess it couldn't decide whether to be a diner or a restaurant. Looking at the outside, you will think it should have stayed a diner. Once you enter, you will know it always did. It is an Auburn landmark and was owned by Bob and Louise Hunter. They were the parents of Neilia Hunter, who married Vice President Joe Biden in 1966. Mrs. Biden was killed in an automobile accident on December 18, 1972. The Biden family still makes occasional visits to the oddly named Dinerant.

Route 20 isn't the only main Upstate thoroughfare with memorable diners. Just the mention of the Roscoe Diner sets one's mouth to watering. It is probably because of the big, fat, juicy dill pickles that the waitress plops down at your table with your menu. Or maybe the revolving refrigerated cake display that greets you at the front door, loaded with cartoonishly big homemade cakes. Or the stacked pastrami sandwiches, which always beg a take-out box to bring the rest home with you. The diner, which opened its doors in 1961, is known to many as "the halfway diner" because thousands of college students who traverse Route 17 between Upstate and New York City know they are almost at the midpoint of their trip when they see the Roscoe Diner at the next exit.

With a daughter going to college in far northern Canton, I had to find a home there for my diner cravings. Diners are few and far between in the North Country, but they do exist, and there are some great ones. One of my favorites is Phillips Diner in Ogdensburg, which has been open on Ford Street since 1948. It is a tiny, comfortable old dining car that has been serving up eggs and hash browns (as well as the local favorite, poutine) to residents and St. Lawrence River visitors alike for three generations. It began life as the Theater Dining Car, serving patrons of the Strand Theater, and it has been in the Phillips family since it first opened its doors. The last time I was there I noticed old suitcases stacked up in the overhead luggage racks above the counter!

The Miss Albany Diner was a favorite haunt of mine while I was attending college in the state's capital in the 1960s. Located in the warehouse district of downtown Albany, this tiny railroad car look-alike eventually rose from supporting role to headliner status. The Miss Albany Diner opened its doors in 1941, and was so well established as a popular bridge to the past that it was chosen to star in several scenes of the 1987 Jack Nicholson movie *Ironweed*, which was filmed in and around Albany. Sadly, the diner closed in 2012. It resurfaced as Sciortino's Italian Restaurant a short time later. Yes, it is still tiny, and yes, it retains all of the old sentimental nuances of the 1940s. And yes, believe it or not, the Italian food is excellent. Photos of Nicholson and co-star Meryl Streep filming scenes of *Ironweed* can be spotted on the walls of the restaurant.

Diners are unique in that, many times, the smaller they are the more memorable they are. There is just something nice about sitting at a counter elbow-to-elbow with a stranger, trying to triple fold the morning paper so as not to get it in each other's eggs, while a bouncy waitress peddles nonstop back and forth behind the counter filling up the morning joes. I used to hate this sunrise pageant, but now that there is no smoking in restaurants, I find it rather convivial in a Mayberry kind of way.

Two microscopic Upstate diners come quickly to mind. I have eaten at both of them. They are wonderful.

The Cooperstown Diner may be the smallest diner in Upstate. In fact it is so small that it has a "½" in its Main Street address! I think the seating capacity is about two dozen. Total. It has been around for as long as anyone can remember. The food is great (including maple milk shakes), and a whole coterie of locals descends on it each morning for coffee and gab.

The Caboose Diner in Norwich sits right next to its former home—the railroad tracks! The diner started out circa 1915 as a working caboose and is now a tiny, but nostalgic, working diner. In a tribute to its former status, a popular item on the menu here is Railroad Toast. Two slices of buttered bread with holes cut in the center and eggs cooked inside the holes.

Of course, there are many hundreds of other diners spread from the Hudson Valley to the High Peaks to Western New York. Big ones and little ones. Each, in its own way, a sentimental looking glass to step through. Each a slice of yesteryear, and each like going on a quick visit "back home."

When I was growing up in Sidney, New York, my life was surrounded by memorable diners. As I grew up in a little factory town in the far northern corner of Delaware County, I found my love for diners nurtured and encouraged by places named Reed's, Ken's, and the Dairy Bar-N.

Just up the road from me was the Unadilla Diner. This was perhaps the quintessential roadside diner of my youth. Located in a community known as the Village Beautiful, the Unadilla Diner had it all. Silvery wings on the outside, colored neon lights above the menu board, red swivel stools, comfortable booths, blue plate specials, and bubbling jukeboxes. The friendly, snappy waitresses always remembered your name after the first time you ate there. Breakfasts were "a dollar something" and the daily specials were "two something" and always came slathered in homemade gravy.

Unadilla sits on Route 7, which runs from Binghamton to Albany. Truckers stopped at the diner like clockwork, locals formed loose knit coffee klatches, farmers came in for an air-conditioning break, and families came in after Sunday church for a hearty breakfast with a soft landing on the wallet.

It was a beautiful place. I mean, real beauty. Shiny, sparkly, clean as a baby's rap sheet. The owners were Larry and Harriet Henchey. They became like family. Harriet, beautiful, theatrical, and broad of gesture. Larry, a chatty and avuncular grill cook, always friendly to the groups of young people who filed in the front door. It was a memorable TV sitcom kind of a diner.

Sadly, it has been closed for years. The Unadilla Diner sits forlornly today on Main Street in the Village Beautiful beckoning passersby to stop for a minute, for a cup, for a chat. Its fading beauty still harkens back to the glory days of yesteryear. I think over time even the For Sale sign has come unglued from the window and has fallen out of sight. I guess people don't want to buy a diner anymore. "Hey, young fella, wanna buy a diner?"

It reminds me of the quote from the movie *The Graduate*. "Just one word: plastics."

Ralph Goings is perhaps the premier photorealism painter in America today. His paintings are as close to an actual photograph as can be humanly possible. His works have been displayed in the Whitney, the Guggenheim, the Museum of Modern Art and other prestigious art galleries and museums. One of his most acclaimed series of paintings involved the interiors of old diners. He crossed the country looking for the most distinctly American roadside diners he could find.

One of his most famous, painted in 1981, is of my favorite but long-gone Unadilla Diner.

THE UPSTATE NEW YORK
FOOD HALL OF FAME

Having lived most of my life near the National Baseball Hall of Fame in Cooperstown, I have often wondered about that very first induction class. Five players were chosen three years before the actual Hall of Fame even opened its doors. But who could have picked them? Out of the thousands of players that had batted and pitched and thrown and stolen and run the bases for decades before 1936. Who didn't make it? And why? Was it a difficult decision?

It's fun, isn't it?

Imagine being on the induction committee. No matter the behind-the-scenes squabbling that must have gone on, few today would argue with the names that emerged triumphant to christen the Hall: Johnson, Cobb, Wagner, Mathewson, and Babe Ruth.

Imagine the conundrum of coming up with the very first inductees in any Hall of Fame. Take basketball in 1959, for example. George Mikan, basketball's first superstar, was a shoo-in. The Football Hall of Fame opened its doors in 1963 welcoming its first class, including Sammy Baugh, Red Grange, and Jim Thorpe. One of the first horses inducted into Saratoga's Racing Hall of Fame was the great Kingston, who finished out of the money only four times in 138 races. Among the first to go in the Hockey Hall was Lord Stanley of "cup fame"; and in tennis it was Bob Wrenn, the first left-handed player to win a U.S. Singles Championship.

What fun, and how difficult, it would have been to sit on the panel picking the very first, the top, the supreme personalities in each sport warranting the initial induction into a Hall of Fame. And it goes way beyond sport. Think of the thankless task it must have been to pick the first women to go in to the Comedy Hall of Fame (no, not Lucille Ball but instead country comic Minnie Pearl). The first class into the Automotive Hall of Fame (Henry Ford, Walter Chrysler). The first group into the Radio Hall of Fame (Groucho Marx, Arthur Godfrey, and Amos 'n' Andy). The Toy Hall of Fame (Barbie, Play-Doh and Crayola Crayons). The Circus Hall of Fame (Lillian Leitzel, a circus strongwoman). The International Towing and Recovery Hall of Fame (Charlie Malcolm, who ran a towing business for fifty years). And so on and so on.

So this leads me to add to the pantheon of great halls of fame in the country by initiating the Upstate New York Food Hall of Fame. Like the founders of other illustrious halls, I have had quite a chore coming up with the initial class. Let me explain how I chose the first five members in America's newest Hall of Fame.

First: place recognition. When you say jambalaya you immediately think of Louisiana. No question. Think Rice-a-Roni? Yup, the San Francisco treat. How about a Kansas City steak? Or a Florida orange? Or an Indiana cornfield? A Maine lobster? Or a Georgia peach? The name recognition just immediately goes to these places when you think of these foods. I mean, do you ever think of a West Virginia peach? Or an Alaska cornfield? Or Rice-a-Roni, a

San Antonio treat? No. So I wanted there to be no mistaking where our first five foods come from no matter where you mentioned them. And that place of course would be Upstate New York.

Second: history. Each of the first five inductees into our hall has a great story. And notice how the stories all seem to swirl around immigrants and their own narratives. I like that. It is just so, I don't know, New Yorky.

Third: loyalty. You will see that passions run high when each of the five inductees is mentioned. People love them. Rivals appear and just as quickly disappear. Thousands of fans populate the Facebook pages and social media outlets of these inductees. Loyalty is worn on the sleeves of a million and more customers. These five nominees are here to stay!

Fourth: familiarity. There are several foods in this book I daresay you have never heard of. But these particular five inductees need no introduction. They have been written about, sung about, filmed, parodied, and loved by millions. The Food Network and every major food magazine have covered all of them extensively. The Wall Street Journal has written about them. YouTube has hundreds of videos pertaining to them. They have been shilled by everybody from Bill Cosby to Popeye's gluttonous best friend.

Number five is that something intangible that just lifts our inductees above all the rest. These are America's favorites. All of them. One is a snack first prepared by an Indian chef in a ritzy Adirondack resort. Another is the most famous food ever to come out of Buffalo. Another is our favorite sandwich. Two are iconic desserts.

They all have great stories. And they all represent Upstate New York proudly on the tables, ice cream parlors, station wagon tailgates, restaurant menus, and backyard patios of America.

To be sure, there are plenty of "pretenders to the throne" when it comes to Upstate food royalty. Skeptics may question *whether Upstate is the true birthplace of each of these first five. But, despite any and all comers who may challenge their pedigrees, as a proud native Upstater I choose to call our region home to them all, and I will let others attempt to claim them for themselves.*

So may I present the first of the initial class for induction into the Upstate New York Food Hall of Fame!

36

THE HAMBURGER
Hamburg

There is just something about a hamburger.

Like our favorite ice cream stand or the pizza parlor of our youth, the best hamburger many of us ever tasted is the one we had when we were sixteen years old. It was usually at a place with a neon sign in the window blinking "Open" and high-backed leatherette booths that friends would squeeze into shoulder to shoulder. The jukebox would be blaring, and the burger would be the common bond that united the sexes, the age differences, and the school rivalries.

For me that place was the Welcome Inn. Sounds like the name of a sitcom. Kind of a cross between *Happy Days* and *Alice*. The Welcome Inn sat near the border of Otsego and Chenango counties in Central New York on Route 7. I started going there in about 1959 and continued until it closed a quarter century later.

The hamburger at the Welcome Inn was the mythic burger of my youth. It was not fancy, it wasn't trendy, and it was not pricey. It was just a chunk of freshly grilled ground beef shoved in between the halves of a Kaiser roll. No condiments, toppings, or sides were served. It was known far and wide as just a "burger on homemade." My generation packed the place on weekend nights throughout my high school years. And, as I have mentioned, although it was not anybody's version of haute cuisine, it was and remains the most memorable burger of my life. I was a teenager on the precipice of life, and my friends and I sorted out all of the world's problems fifty years ago in a torn red leatherette booth at the Welcome Inn in Bainbridge.

191

Tom (left) and John Menches are direct descendants of the inventor of the hamburger. (Photo courtesy of Menches Brothers Restaurant, www.menchesbros.net)

Regrettably, the Welcome Inn remains only in my dreams. But it is a wonderful dream.

So what is it about a hamburger, and where did this simple, sentimental yet powerful sandwich come from?

I wish I believed that the hamburger was born in New Haven, Connecticut. I really do.

There, on Crown Street, you will find Louis' Lunch, established in 1895 and proclaimed as "the birthplace of the hamburger." Louis Lassen is credited with being the first person to throw some grilled meat between two slices of bread. The tiny sandwich shop still flame broils its meat patties over an 1898 cast iron gas stove. It is one of New Haven's most popular landmarks.

So why do I wish it were true that the burger began here? Because those who do believe it actually have a destination, a birthplace, a temple to visit and worship to the gods of the hamburger. Tourists flock to Louis' Lunch, crowd the sidewalk out front to get their photograph taken with the eatery in the background, take home menus as souvenirs, and enter the front door as if they were entering the hallowed inner sanctum of a shrine. Tour guides point to it as one of New Haven's great icons.

All of the major television food programs have filmed at Louis' Lunch, with the Travel Channel actually dubbing it "the tastiest burger in America." Most authorities, including the Library of Congress, have acknowledged that this was in fact the place that the hamburger was born.

And that is why I wish I believed it too. Because I also get that special kick out of actually going to the out-of-the-way historic landmarks, food or otherwise.

But, let's face it. It's in New Haven, Connecticut.

And that is why *this* Upstater throws his lot in with the Menches brothers of Western New York. Charlie and Frank Menches first sold their own version of grilled meat sandwiches at the Erie County Fair in Hamburg, NY, in 1885. The two were clever, untiring, energetic innovators (they would later invent the waffle ice cream cone).

Local legend has it that they ran out of their sausage product at the fair one day and started substituting beef in between the roll halves, and a legend was born. It was not an easy decision, however. It is important to remember that a century ago fairs and expositions were considered to be one of the high points of the social calendar. People actually got dressed up to visit a fair. Men in suits and bowler hats carried parasols over the dainty heads of the women strolling alongside of them. These genteel ladies were resplendent in dresses, bustles, and gloves. Formal wear at a county fair? Always.

The Erie County Fair (then hosted by the Erie County Agricultural Society) was no common fair. It was one of the largest summer social gatherings in America and, being located just south of Buffalo, which at the time was one of the ten most populous cities in the nation, the fair welcomed visitors of every social standing including bluebloods, millionaires, and celebrities.

Realizing that no ordinary, bland beef patty would do, Charlie Menches concocted a clever way to make the brothers' first attempt at grilled meat more interesting, more flavorful, and more acceptable to the exotic tastes of the upper crust as well as the hoi polloi. He gathered up some spices from the kitchen and mixed them into the beef. He then added brown sugar and dark coffee for flavor and coloring and grilled it up. It was a hit.

When that first customer chomped down on that first burger in 1885, he quizzed the Menches as to what it was called. Local legend has it that their sandwich stand at the fair was located near the town's water tower, which read "Hamburg." Sensing history in the making, Menches declared, "That, sir, is a hamburger."

So that should settle the age-old question, "Which came first, the sandwich or the town?"

"My great-great-grandfather was Charles Menches, and my great-great-uncle was Frank," Tom Menches, sixty-six, told me. "They were sausage concessionaires from Ohio who just happened to run out of product at the Hamburg Fair. It is as simple as that. They invented the hamburger."

Tom is prideful of his family's role in the birth of an American food institution. "They had taken their sausage stands to various fairs all around, including the big World's Fairs in Chicago and St. Louis. They were very popular fellas and were in fact friends with President William McKinley," Menches told me. "When they ran out of sausage up in Hamburg they went to a butcher and had him grind up some beef for them. My great-great-grandfather thought the meat was too bland to sell so he added some brown sugar and coffee to make it tastier and a more appealing color. And that is how it started."

The Menches name and claim does not come without some scars. "Oh sure, there are several other people who claim that they invented the hamburger. But we believe it belongs to our family," Tom told me.

If we assume that the timeline for a hamburger in America begins with the Mencheses' stand at the Erie County Fair in 1885 (as any true Upstater *should* believe), it is interesting to acknowledge the many other "inventors" who also claimed to make the first burger in the nation. Like "Hamburger Charlie" Nagreen. He came along later in the same summer as the Menches brothers. He flattened his meatballs to make them easier to carry around the Seymour (Wisconsin) County Fair. Wisconsinites claim Hamburger Charlie as the inventor of the hamburger, and to ward off any naysayers they recently erected a full color twelve-foot tall statue of Hamburger Charlie in downtown Seymour.

Believe it or not, by government decree, the state of Oklahoma declares itself the "birthplace of the American hamburger" due to reports that Okie Oscar Bilby served up the sandwich to his farm workers in 1891. Fletcher Davis of Athens, Texas, is another frustrated claimant. Historians in his home area continue to scramble for evidence of his invention in the 1880s. But while that search continues, plaques have been erected in his honor, hamburger festivals are held in his name, and in 2006 the Texas Legislature passed a resolution declaring Ol' Fletch to be the "father of the American Hamburger."

So despite all the hoopla and the passions and the fact and fiction, somebody had to do it the first time. And so for this reason, I submit the names of Charles and Frank Menches for nomination as the inventors of our first Upstate New York Food Hall of Fame member—the hamburger.

As I said, I am disappointed that Upstate has no remaining brick-and-mortar touchstones to the Menches' first creation. I've been to Louis' in Connecticut, where I paid homage to Charlie and Frank's nearest competitor for the crown. And you can go and see the fairly creepy, gigantic "hamburger man" in Seymour, Wisconsin. But what about us Upstaters? Where do we go?

Ohio, actually.

Massillon or Green, Ohio, to be exact. Here you will find the Menches Brothers Restaurants, opened up by Tom and John Menches, the great-great-grandsons of the inventors. Both venues are popular full-service restaurants that tell the story of the birth of the hamburger in 1885.

"A lot of people come into the restaurant and see the old photographs and read our little history cards and they just can't believe that a relative of ours invented the hamburger. And we make them with the same recipe as Charles Menches did a century and a half ago, brown sugar, coffee and all!"

I asked Tom how he felt about all of the other claimants to the title of Inventor of the Hamburger.

"Well, funny thing," he began. "One time a few years back the city of Akron got all the families together in a mock court to find out who was the real inventor of the hamburger. They had a judge and everything. We had our own family there as did the Lassens from Louis' Lunch. Relatives of Hamburger Charlie came in from Wisconsin and some folks came up from Texas representing the Davis family. All the major families involved were there. It was great fun and everyone came out for the 'trial.'"

I asked Tom who the court decided was the real inventor of the hamburger.

"It was a hung jury," he laughed. "So we went ahead and claimed the title. I mean where did Hamburger Charlie come up with the name for his sandwich? He had never been to Hamburg, New York, and was rolling meatballs for goodness sake," Tom chuckled. "Oh well, it gets people talking. I tell the other families that they can claim to have invented the cheeseburger. But the hamburger, well, that belongs to the Mencheses."

It is an interesting footnote to also recognize New York State as the birthplace of the hot dog, arguably America's second most popular sandwich. Most people think the hot dog was invented by Nathan's of Coney Island. Close. But not close enough.

The American hot dog (known as a frankfurter) was first served up by Charles Feltman on Coney Island. The restaurateur decided to place a sausage in a bun around 1870 to bypass having to give out expensive utensils and plates with his meals. One of his employees, Nathan Handwerker, would soon leave Feltman's employ and go into successful competition for the hot dog business along the Coney Island boardwalk.

Hamburgers and hot dogs. Two of America's favorite meals. Both invented by immigrants who named their creations after a German city. Both sandwiches are native to New York.

Unfortunately for the hot dog, though, it was not created Upstate so its day of glorious induction will have to wait until someone comes up with a *Downstate* New York Food Hall of Fame. If it is any reconciliation to frankfurter fanatics, though, the hot dog does have its very own chapter in this book.

So the hamburger of my youth is long gone, the oldest burger place in America is in GPS-land somewhere in Connecticut, and the heirs to hamburger royalty reside in Massillon, Ohio. Where am I to go in Upstate New York to find a memorable burger, a place with a long family history, and a place that gives me the sense that I am back with my friends at the Welcome Inn?

That place resides just an echo south of the tallest waterfall east of the Rocky Mountains.

The Glenwood Pines Restaurant is located in the Town of Ulysses in Tompkins County. It is just south of the historic Taughannock Falls State Park (hence the echo reference) and four miles north of Ithaca. It sits on an aerie overlooking Cayuga Lake. The place is small, rustic, and totally familiar.

"My dad and granddad bought this place with my aunt and uncle on Valentine's Day 1979. They are all Hohwalds, and I am the most recent family member to take over this place," Corey Hohwald told me. He is the present manager of Glenwood Pines.

"It was just a small gin mill at the time. It was originally owned by the Evans family who still lives across the road from the restaurant. They had a farm and built this to be their dairy stand," Corey told me.

After nearly four decades of Hohwald stewardship, Glenwood Pines has earned a special niche in the hearts of Central New Yorkers from several miles around. The place is woodsy and a little old fashioned, which is a plus. There is a definite whiff of nostalgia when you walk in the front door. The knotty pine walls, the kitschy bric-a-brac all over the place (they have a special affinity for bobble head dolls here, and they will gladly let you peruse their collection of more than four hundred on display), the whole everybody-knows-your-name kind of aura to it. One wall is lined with old video and arcade games. Want to play one of the original Pac Man games or throw one of those old silver pucks down a polished lane at some electronic bowling pins? They got them.

And the place is spotless.

"We pride ourselves on being a typical type of restaurant that you can bring the whole family to. Our prices are reasonable, our style is most definitely casual and we are proud of our heritage at Glenwood Pines," Corey told me. "Plus, we make one terrific hamburger."

I ordered up a Pinesburger, their classic favorite. It came just as I ordered it, charbroiled and grilled exactly to my medium-well specifics. It was topped with fresh garnish and came with a large order of French fries. The healthy-sized, six-ounce, hand-pressed patty was served on a miniloaf of fresh French bread baked at the local Ithaca Bakery.

"The big difference here is that our meat comes in fresh in large USDA Grade A boneless beef chuck shoulder clods. We carve it up, grind it ourselves, and hand-form each patty. We have been making the Pinesburger the same way for decades, and people have made it their favorite."

That is an understatement.

A back wall of the restaurant is lined with numerous certificates and awards declaring the Pinesburger, and the restaurant as a whole, the best in the area. One certificate reads "Winner of the Best Burger Award, 1995." There are many other "best burger" awards that followed it. Another names it "The Best Restaurant to Bring Kids To, 1999." Another trumpets their "Best Fish Fry." The awards just go on and on.

"Even though we have a rather small kitchen area, we have served as many as six hundred people here on a busy Saturday night. And most of them order the Pinesburger. Sometimes 350 burgers in a single evening."

"Our clientele runs the gamut from six to eighty-six. Since we are close to Ithaca we get a lot of students and professors in from Cornell. It is amazing during Cornell graduation weekend. Grandfathers will bring their newly cap-and-gowned grandchild in here and tell them about how they used to come here themselves for a Pinesburger years ago. And it is a fun place. We don't take ourselves too seriously."

Corey and his staff, including his Uncle Ken, are always coming up with fun ideas to keep the customers, mostly locals, happy. They'll throw a Hawaiian night or an ugly Christmas sweater contest that brings in large crowds of hungry fun seekers.

"We recently tried a Flannel Friday. Everybody got a special deal if they came in wearing flannel," he laughed. "It was wall-to-wall flannel in here on the first night, including all my staff. We had a great time."

They offer a food challenge here at Glenwood Pines. If you could eat four Pinesburgers in a one-hour sitting, you used to receive a free T-shirt and your photo would go up on the restaurant's Wall of Fame.

"We still do it but we had to stop displaying the photos," he told me. "I guess it is just too easy to do. At last count more than four thousand people have conquered the Pinesburger Challenge, so we ran out of room for all the photographs!"

Glenwood Pines sits on a bluff "high above Cayuga's waters." The only thing between your Pinesburger and the lake is the Ithaca Yacht Club. In the spring and early winter the vista is wonderful.

I asked Corey, thirty-three, what kind of responsibility he feels to be in charge of such a longstanding family business.

"Every day I feel that responsibility. I give a good quality product that people love, and we have a nice, friendly place here. When I was a baby my parents put me in a crib at the end of the bar while they tended to this place. I started out sweeping the floors and cleaning the place before I was ten when school was on break. I now manage it. I always remind myself to not let them down. My dad and grandfather and Aunt Deb and Uncle Ken put it all in many years ago to make a go of this place. I honor them by keeping the tradition strong. I obviously love this place, the staff and the customers, and, when it comes right down to it, it is a fun place to work."

After polishing off the last of my Pinesburger, I kidded Corey to come up with one fun highlight of his years at Glenwood Pines.

"Well, believe it or not, we have had the hockey Stanly Cup in here on three different occasions. Ithaca is a big hockey town. Joe Nieuwendk, a Cornell graduate and member of the NHL Hall of Fame, won the Stanley Cup three times and brought the trophy in here a couple of times. They were kind of low key affairs.

"But when Dustin Brown, who was actually born in Ithaca, won his Stanley Cup with the Los Angeles Kings in 2012, he returned home with the trophy and came here to the restaurant. And that night was anything but a low key affair," Corey said. "He'd been here before and had eaten the Pinesburger many times. He arrived in a stretch limousine with an entourage of more than forty people. Since he was a hometown boy our restaurant was packed with well-wishers. He came wading through the crowd with the big silver Stanley Cup trophy and everybody just let out a roar. It was very exciting."

So what did he do with the trophy once he was inside?

"He put it up on the bar, filled it with Labatt's Blue and drank from it," he laughed.

Corey walked me out to my car where we once again admired the view over Cayuga Lake one last time. He shook my hand, gave me a slap on the back and said, "Come back again some time."

As I drove away I felt like I had just revisited the Welcome Inn of my youth and had eaten the "burger on homemade" of my dreams.

37

CHICKEN WINGS

Buffalo

*A*ll Hail the Queen!

What a glorious day it was back on March 4, 1964, when Teressa Bellissimo first tossed a forlorn chicken wing into a deep fryer, coated it with some hot sauce, and served it up to her son Dominic and his partying friends. It was a hit with the young partiers and the word soon spread that something special was cooking down at the Anchor Bar, 1047 Main Street in downtown Buffalo. This gastronomical act by the Queen of the Chicken Wings opened up the doors for a world-wide phenomenon now known as America's favorite appetizer, the Buffalo hot wing.

To put this sensation in perspective, one must remember that the chicken wing was an anonymous, nondescript item before that fateful March night in 1964. I myself grew up in my father's grocery and butcher shop. I watched him cut up thousands of chickens over his years, always focusing only on the meaty, juicy body of the bird. Impaling them on the stainless steel skewers of the rotisserie oven where thirty at a time they would go round and round like a delectable carnival attraction until they were browned and seasoned to perfection. My father would then slide them off their individual swords and serve them up to an eager line of customers. As a kid, my job was to reach into the twirling rotisserie and sprinkle the sizzling birds with paprika to "give them that special Don's Market touch," as my Dad would say.

But where was the rest of the chicken? The parts to the whole?

In the garbage.

Duff's manager, Ed Conley, has been serving up hot wings in Buffalo for more than twenty-five years. Here he is standing in front of a photo display of President Obama's visit to Duff's.

I remember back in the 1950s, my dad had a heck of a time trying to sell or even give away the parts of the chicken left over from his artful carvings. Wings? Useless. Necks? Maybe for a soup stock for Cora Landers or Pearl Couse. Hearts? Gross. Gizzards? Don't even go there.

Today the Anchor Bar is known around the world as the birthplace of the hot wing. Nary a tourist nor a motor coach can come through Buffalo without having to stop for a wing at Teressa's place. It is just what you do. While most cities have a logo or icon representing them that reflects on their founding, their creation, or their early American roots, I dare say nobody would mind if the official emblem for the city of Buffalo was a dancing chicken wing. I am serious. Chicken wings are as closely associated with the city as are the Buffalo Bills or a hard winter.

So again, all hail the Queen! And aren't we all glad that Teressa Bellissimo had a bucket of chicken wings handy that night in 1964 rather than a bucket of chicken gizzards?

While recognizing the Anchor Bar for all its fame and glory, I would submit that a place in the Upstate New York Food Hall of Fame should be saved for another legendary Buffalo wing, the one served out at Duff's on Sheridan Drive.

Here you can get one of the best plates of hot wings you'll find anywhere in New York.

"A few years after the Anchor Bar came up with the deep fried chicken wing, our founder, Louise Duffney, decided to try it out here. And by 'out here' I mean out in the boondocks," Ed Conley told me. He is the manager of the original Duff's Famous Wings. "Back in 1969 when Louise first served up her own wings with her special sauce, we were a long way out from downtown Buffalo. We are actually in Amherst, so now we are just a suburb of the city, but back then we were nothing but farms and wide open spaces. Really a ghost town. Louise had a gin mill here at this very location, and she decided to try the wings for her patrons. They really liked them, I guess, because before long she was going through a full case of chicken wings a week."

Duff's now goes through seventy-five thousand chicken wings *a week*!

The place is a snow globe of nostalgia. A medium sized dining room, a small bar, old black-and-white photos of Duff's growth over the years on the walls, and a friendly wait staff that makes you feel like a regular, even if it is your first visit to Duff's. Ed Conley oversees the whole place with an unassuming cordiality and neighborliness that he seems born into.

"I have been here for almost twenty-five years," he told me. "I've watched this place grow through a couple of generations of customers. I just love it when parents bring their kids in here and tell them about 'how they used to come here when they were kids themselves.' The University of Buffalo is nearby, and students have been coming in here forever. It is a nice mix of old and young. People love this place. It's not too big and not too small. It's just right," he laughed.

Duff's has been crowded into the tight corner of Sheridan Drive and Millersport Road by shopping malls and ever widening thoroughfares. Extra room for parking at Duff's stopped a decade ago. What you see is what you get, and it can be problematic. But no matter where you have to park, the reward is certainly well worth it.

The wings here are simply awesome.

"We only serve them crisp. We leave them in the fryer a little longer than most places do, and that is what sets us apart from the other wing places," Ed said. "Our sauces come from Louise's original recipe from 1969, and we serve them in various degrees of heat: mild, hot, suicide, and death. When we say our hot wings are hot, we mean it. Medium is our best seller but we still have folks who come in and try and challenge themselves with the ones on the extreme end of hot. We serve all our wings with bleu cheese, celery, and carrots. We serve burgers and all kinds of sandwiches, but obviously we are known for our wings," he said as he pointed to the now full dining room. There was a pile of deep red wings in a bowl on virtually every table.

Everybody has a favorite wing place, no matter whether you live in New York City or San Francisco or Houston. But here in Buffalo, the birthplace of the wing, the loyalties to this dish run deep and strong.

So who has the best hot wing in Buffalo?

"It is impossible to name the best wing because everybody has a favorite, but we certainly think ours are far and above the best wings in the city," the manager told me.

"Is that because you work here and have probably had your fair share of Duff's wings over the years?" I kidded him.

"No, not really. But here are a couple of examples as to why I think we are the best. Besides the long lines out the door on weekends, of course.

"In 2010, President Obama came to Buffalo for an afternoon visit. The White House would not tell anyone where exactly the president was going to make stops in the city, but everybody assumed that since Mr. Obama was a consummate politician, he'd certainly have some of the city's favorite wings while he was here. Most of the focus, frankly, was on the Anchor Bar because of its historical importance. Well, what do you know? We got a call that he was coming to our Cheektowaga Duff's. Everybody jumped to it and, before long, in walks President Obama and his staff, entourage, and press pool right here into Duff's," Ed laughed.

"We were thrilled. He came in and greeted everyone, posed for a lot of photos, and ordered up some lunch. Several customers offered the president their tables so he could sit down, but he refused. He just didn't want to bother them."

"So what did he order," I inquired.

"Ten medium wings, some onion rings and an order of French fries. When he couldn't decide on fries or onion rings, our bartender looked up at him and said, 'You are the president. Order them both.' And he did! He got his order to go and ate them in his limo on the way to his next stop. Yup, that was a big day for Duff's, and of course it was on the front page of all the papers," he told me as we walked into a little room covered with framed items.

And right in the center of the crowded wall, surrounded by countless Best Wings in Buffalo awards and plaques, is a large photo of President Barack Obama chowing down on some Duff's hot wings.

"Also in 2010, we had a *real* showdown," Ed began. "The Travel Channel *Food Wars* show came to Buffalo for a big confrontation between two wing restaurants for the bragging rights of the best wings in the city. It was all in good fun, but what an exciting day it was. They pitted Duff's against the Anchor Bar. On Saturday, they came here and we served them up a plate of our best. Then they went down to the Anchor Bar and they did the same. Then on Sunday a panel of five judges got together to discuss and vote on the result. And this was all on national television."

I could hardly wait for the answer.

"We won, 3–2," Ed said with a loud laugh. "Yessir, the best wings in Buffalo. What a time that was."

Duff's is a place that is hard to describe. It is a throwback to the old days of drive-ins and mom-and-pop family eateries, yet Duff's is jarringly scrunched in between high-end department stores and glittery, neon-faced automobile showrooms. It is warm and familiar and welcoming the minute you enter the front door. The booths are "let's-get-comfortable" cozy, and the pace is "let's-sit-for-a-while" unhurried. The wait staff is personable and unobtrusive.

And the wings?

Well, for a wing nut like me who likes a bite to the sauce, likes a place steeped in history, enjoys hot wings only on the crispy side, and will always strive to go to any place that serves "the best in the city," I have only one word for Duff's wings.

Unforgettable.

38

JELL-O
LeRoy

*I*t is quite an achievement when a product becomes so universal, so widely known, that it actually becomes a generic term for any other product of its kind. Kleenex, for example. If you need a nose tissue you always ask for a Kleenex no matter what other brand is handy. We all clean our ears with Q-tips even though there are many other ear-cleaning swabs by other names. When we need to copy things we ask to Xerox them; when we get a boo-boo we put a Band-Aid on it; and when we have leftover meat loaf we put it in a Ziploc bag. Your doctor tells you to take two aspirins and call him in the morning. He doesn't say take two Dr. Wilson's relief tablets and call him, even if that is what you end up buying.

Imagine the frustration of going into the reusable plastic bag business. Today? Or opening up your own medicated adhesive strip store? Why bother? They'll only come in asking for Ziploc bags and Band-Aids anyway.

Jell-O is the same thing. Since 1842, it has risen to become the generic name for any flavored gelatin dessert.

Peter Cooper had the original patent for powdered gelatin. You remember him, don't you? He is the same man who gave America its first steam-powered locomotive, the Tom Thumb. Cooper held on to the gelatin patent for a few years trying to figure out how to market the stuff. Imagine how hard it must have been to try and soften up the image of a product that was basically a conglomeration of everything that the butcher left on the butcher block, including muscle, intestines, and boiled bones.

Yummy.

LeRoy's Jell-O Museum tells the story of a runaway marketing success, thanks to ads by graphic design icons like Norman Rockwell.

Pearle Wait bought the patent in 1885, and it was his wife, Mary, who decided to add flavors to the product and gave it its funny name. Hence Jell-O was born, all four flavors of it: strawberry, raspberry, lemon, and orange. In 1899, Jell-O was bought by Orator Woodward, a food processor from western New York, for $450. Jell-O was made in LeRoy for many years.

This is the LeRoy connection, and this is where Jell-O began its international march to fame and, well, generic destiny.

Jell-O is today far and away the most popular dessert gelatin in the world. Billions of boxes of the jiggly treat have been sold since Woodward began employing his formidable marketing skills to product. Through cookbooks, free handouts, celebrity endorsements, an elaborate advertising campaign, and just plain hucksterism (he called it "America's Most Famous Dessert," when it was hardly so), the name Jell-O is now recognized in virtually every country on the globe.

LeRoy is a town of about eight thousand residents in Genesee County. They honor the fame of its most well-known export in many ways, not the least being the Jell-O Museum. Here visitors will find themselves sur-rounded by dazzling, colorful Jell-O boxes scattered through the roomy, modern facility. These jewel boxes illustrate the changes in the packag-ing down through the decades. Old advertisements featuring the original artwork of an astonishing array of America's earliest, most famous graphic artists line the walls. Here you will see Norman Rockwells hanging next to Maxfield Parrishes, which are hanging next to Jell-O advertisements drawn by Rose O'Neil, who gave America the Kewpie Doll.

One of the oddest and, frankly, most fun displays at the museum is the Jell-O Brain.

On March 17, 1993, St. Jerome Hospital in Batavia, NY, sent several technicians to the Jell-O Museum to conduct a forensic study. For years there had been stories told that the electricity produced from a simple Jell-O mold was similar to brain waves emitted by a human being. At the risk of pre-empting a visit by you to this wonderful museum, let me just say the results on display are remarkable.

Comedian Bill Cosby, the longtime pitchman for Jell-O, actually vis-ited little LeRoy once. The whole town came out to see the superstar comedian, and he didn't disappoint. When he reached the top of the stairs entering the museum he turned to the crowd and yelled out, "I was eat-ing Jell-O before I was paid to eat Jell-O!" The crowd, of course, roared. Cosby's forty-year spokesman connection with Jell-O is believed to be the most enduring celebrity endorsement affiliation ever.

The LeRoy Historical Society museum is located in front of the Jell-O Museum. The two are connected by the "Jell-O Brick Road," a walkway with inscribed pavers honoring donors to the museum.

Bill Cosby's paver reads: "To Bill Cosby. Thanks for 30 Years of Jell-O Giggles. June 8, 2004."

At one time Jell-O was such a part of the American imprint that it was actually served up to immigrants passing through Ellis Island as a "wel-come to America" gesture. There are currently more than twenty different flavors of Jell-O (strawberry remains the top seller), and Jell-O molds hold-ing everything from fruits and nuts to pine needles have graced backyard picnic tables for more than a century.

As old fashioned as the idea of this simple flavored gelatin is, young people today have turned to it en masse for an even more creative use than say a Jell-O Pretzel Salad or even a Slime Lemon Jell-O Cake.

Jell-O shots anybody? Sure, why not? There's always room for Jell-O!

39

ICE CREAM SUNDAE

Ithaca

*N*ot unlike the Hatfields and McCoys, there had been a real shoot 'em up going on for years between two American communities vying for the right to be called the Birthplace of the Ice Cream Sundae.

While there have been other contenders, both Two Rivers, Wisconsin, and Ithaca, New York, were the final two left standing in the ring. Both places claimed birthing rights to the dessert, and a nation watched with mouthwatering glee as historical evidence, publicity campaigns, official proclamations, and government decrees bolstered each city's claim to the prize.

Two Rivers seemed to be ahead by a length as they and Ithaca came down to the imaginary finish line. The city of eleven thousand on the shore of Lake Michigan submitted for public acceptance a lawyer's brief filled with empirical evidence of the birth of the sundae in their fair town in 1881. The state government came stomping in, covering everything up with an official stamp of approval, and in 1973 erected a historical marker proclaiming for the entire world to see that credit for the invention of the ice cream sundae belonged here. It reads:

The Ice Cream Sundae. In 1881 George Hallelauer asked Edward C. Berner, the owner of a soda fountain at 1404 15th Street, to top a dish of ice cream with chocolate sauce, hitherto only used for ice cream sodas. The concoction cost a nickel and soon became very popular. But it was only served on Sundays. One day a ten year old girl insisted she have a dish of ice cream "with that stuff on top" saying they could pretend it was Sunday. After that the confection was served every day in many

Owners Bruce and Heather Lane show off one of their popular ice cream sundaes. Their shop is in Ithaca, where the dessert was born in 1894.

flavors. It lost its Sunday-only association to be called ICE CREAM SUN-
DAE when a glassware salesman placed an order with his company for
the long canoe-shaped dishes in which it was served, as sundae dishes.

The large marker, carrying the emblem of the State of Wisconsin and
erected in Central Park in downtown Two Rivers, sure looks official. The
original Berner's soda fountain was re-created, the main street was fes-
tooned with banners carrying the image of an ice cream sundae, and the
city held festivals and special sundae events throughout the year. So that's
the end of the story, right?

Hold onto your whipped cream. There is more to the story.

Ithaca, located in the Finger Lakes region of Central New York, also
laid claim to the ice cream sundae honor, and the two communities
fought tooth and nail to "out prove" each other. After a protracted public
relations spat, Ithaca came up with the holy grail of evidence: a printed ad

from the *Ithaca Daily Journal* dated April 5, 1892, advertising a "Cherry Sunday, the new ten cent ice cream specialty served only at Platt and Colt's Famous Day and Night Pharmacy in Ithaca."

This remains the earliest written evidence of the invention of the Cherry Sunday.

Cornell University, located in Ithaca, holds in its archives an 1894 letter from Washington, DC, patent lawyer William G. Henderson advising Platt and Colt on trademark options. Henderson, who clearly had never even heard of the dessert, states that the only option for the pharmacy would be to apply for a trademark for international sales. He alludes to the fact that the "ice cream and syrup novelty" is probably not capable of being shipped overseas.

So that settles it for historians. Well, for those of us from Upstate New York anyways. Sorry, Two Rivers. Nice try.

Now I find myself in Ithaca seeking out the best ice cream sundae in the city of its birth. Where to go?

"Our ice cream store is one of the oldest continuously operating of its kind in the region," Bruce Lane told me. His red-and-white nostalgic parlor, Purity Ice Cream, has been sitting just off the downtown Ithaca business district since 1936. It was founded by Cornell grad Leo Guentert and later run by his granddaughter Margo Klose.

"They had a real old-time kind of a family place that became quite successful. It was a friendly place, a gathering spot for families and friends to meet. Over time, I became interested in buying the place, but Margo just wasn't ready to sell yet. I was persistent and asked several times over the years until she finally agreed that it was time. I feel very lucky to own Purity Ice Cream. It's an amazing place," Lane said.

The shop exudes nostalgia, from the flashy *Happy Days* colors right down to the old-fashioned red leather and shiny chrome ambiance. You almost expect to see Fonzie and Richie and Pottsie sitting over in a corner booth.

The menu is stacked with all kinds of ice cream desserts. Obviously, cones are the biggest sellers. "We have very little parking and no drive-up window at all. And yet still on a hot July afternoon, we can easily go through one thousand ice cream cones. It is just a tradition in this area to get a cone or a sundae at Purity. Generations have been coming here, and that is one of the great joys of owning this place," Lane told me.

The flavors run the gamut from "what you'd expect" to "what the heck is that?" Chocolate Debris, Fingerlakes Tourist, Gimme Mocha Fudge, and Sleepers Awake fall into the latter category.

You cannot accuse Bruce Lane of being trapped in amber, living only in the past. "We added a big line of baked goods over the years. We make them ourselves and the public has really responded to them. As is the case with most ice cream parlors in Upstate New York, our business really slows down between Labor Day and Christmas. The baked goods offer a way to keep customers coming in the front door."

So how does it feel to be the oldest ice cream parlor serving ice cream sundaes in the place of their birth?

"It is definitely cool," he answered. "The fact that Ithaca holds claim to that is pretty neat. The city doesn't really 'shout it from the roof top' but we like to honor the tradition of it by serving a big and delicious sundae. In fact we have many varieties of sundaes, and they all are popular."

I relayed to the owner that just sitting in his parlor eating a sundae (which was big, sloppy, and heavenly) felt almost magical. Does he feel that way?

"The fact that I own Purity Ice Cream does have a special meaning to me and my family. The longevity of the product, the high quality standards we use, the hundreds of young people who over the years found their first job here, the generational appeal to our many customers are all important. I really believe that many more people know Purity Ice Cream than know that Ithaca is the home of the sundae. But we are working on that," he chuckled.

The one thing that struck me about this shop, and about nostalgic ice cream parlors in general, is the whole notion of them as a gathering place for friends and family. I asked Bruce about that.

"I am living proof that that is true, Chuck," he replied. "I used to come here all the time as just one of the regular customers. Gathering, if you will, with my friends and family over the years. Eventually, I met a vivacious young business woman named Heather, and we fell in love. One day I brought her here to share an ice cream sundae with me on the patio out front. My two young daughters were with me. Halfway through our sundae, and in front of the big dinner crowd at the parlor, I told Heather I had something to say to her. I got up out of my seat, went over to her, got down on my knee and proposed marriage to her right there in front of everybody. Lucky for me she said yes," he laughed.

"Little did I know that a few years later she and I would own this wonderful place. In fact on the day we closed on purchasing Purity, I said to Heather, 'Well, honey, we now have an ice cream business.'"

I asked what her response was. "She looked up at me and said, 'I'm pregnant.'" Today Bruce and Heather's two sons, Denny and Andy, now both teenagers, work at the shop.

In parting, I noted to Bruce that during our interview the word "fun" had come up several times. I asked him why this was such an enjoyable place to visit and to work at.

"Well, the truth is, Chuck, it's hard to eat an ice cream sundae and be unhappy," he smiled.

40

POTATO CHIPS

Saratoga Springs

The backstory to the birth of the potato chip is as colorful as any in this book. We meet an Indian chef with a whimsical last name, we find a grudge match between a persnickety well-to-do customer and a brother-and-sister culinary team, and it all plays out against the backdrop of one of Upstate's toniest playgrounds for the rich and famous.

"Yes, we love George Crum here in Saratoga," chirped Mary Ann Fitzgerald, the Saratoga Springs City Historian. "Sure, we get plenty of calls about the history of our city, the famous racetrack, the mineral springs which made us famous, and many other subjects. But it is George and his potato chip that people are most fascinated by."

Crum, a Native American / African American chef of high regard, had been employed by many respectable restaurants in the Adirondacks over a number of years. At Moon's Lake House, he was known for serving the finest fried potatoes in the area.

"Now that Lake House was a sight to see," Fitzgerald told me. "It was the fanciest place around, and it sat on an absolutely gorgeous spit of land overlooking Saratoga Lake. You can still see where the old buildings of the resort once were, although today it is a private residence.

"Crum and his sister, Catherine, were the cooks there. Moon's was famous for its French fried potatoes. The oft-told tale was that one day a wealthy diner complained to the chef that his fried potatoes were too thick, and he demanded thinner ones. Crum and his sister were back in the kitchen, and they set out to teach this fussy patron a lesson. George

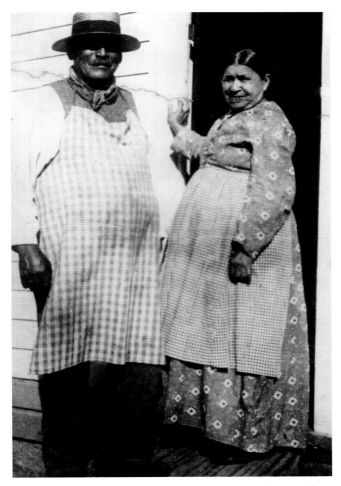

A rare photo of the inventor of the potato chip, Indian chef George Crum, and his sister Katie. (Photo courtesy of George S. Bolster Collection of the Saratoga Springs History Museum)

decided to cut a potato so thin as to not be eaten with a fork. When it was fried and served Crum and his sister peeked out through the kitchen door to watch the man's reaction. To everyone's surprise, the customer loved the new creation. He even ordered more. Soon 'Saratoga Chips' were on the menu and a legend was born," she said.

"Many tell the story that the wealthy customer that fateful day was none other than Cornelius Vanderbilt, a Saratoga regular. But that is all speculation. It was so long ago, and nothing was ever written down. I have compiled a large binder at my office of all the different stories about Mr. Crum and his invention. From tales, lore and stories that have been handed down over the generations. Everybody has their own favorite twist to the legend. It makes it all fun and interesting. But one thing is undeniable. Potato chips were invented in 1853 by George Crum right here at Moon's Lake House in Saratoga Springs," she said with certainty.

Today the potato chip makes up a third of our nation's total snack food consumption, some fifty billion dollars–worth annually.

In the middle of the nineteenth century, Saratoga Springs was called America's Monte Carlo. During the city's Gilded Age, casinos flourished and railroads disgorged a virtual Blue Book of American royalty to descend onto the four-star hotels and restaurants of Broadway, Saratoga's main thoroughfare. Union Avenue was asplash with jaw-dropping Victorian mansions featuring gaily colored awnings, brightly painted turrets, and sweeping manicured front lawns. The famed mineral springs brought international visitors here to experience the "water cure" for what ailed them. The Saratoga Race Course, opened in 1864, was the place to see and to be seen for high-society matrons and commoners alike. It remains the focal point for all Saratoga activity, and is the oldest sporting venue in the United States.

"Saratoga is filled with history of all kinds," Fitzgerald said, "but there is just something so wonderful, so fun about the story of the invention of the potato chip here that people all over the world are fascinated by it. In fact, a few years ago a television movie crew from Germany came and filmed a whole program on George Crum and his potato chip. The title of the film was *Die Kartofflechips des Mr. Crum*," she chuckled.

"We led the crew around the area for a full day. We shot scenes throughout the city, we went into the stores and interviewed people, and visited George's final resting place in Malta Ridge Cemetery. We even went to where the Moon's Landing House resort was on the lake. In fact, the owners of the property let the film crew enter the old building that we believe is the original kitchen of the restaurant where George first tried out his creation. That was pretty special," she sighed.

I reminded Ms. Fitzgerald that I had once done some research on the burial place of George Crum and was stymied by the fact that he changed his last name along the way.

"Yes, you are right Chuck," she told me. "Apparently Mr. Vanderbilt was very fond of Crum and once told him, 'George, you know that a speck is larger than a crumb, don't you?' After that George started calling himself George Speck, and that is the name on his tombstone."

One company keeps George Crum/Speck's flame alive. The Original Saratoga Chips Company brought back the iconic snack in 2009 after it had been forgotten for almost a century. These chips can now be found in most stores or ordered on the company's website.

But, as they say, "When in Rome. . . ."

"If you are in Saratoga Springs you just have to go to the Stadium Café on Broadway," Mary Ann Fitzgerald told me. "The chef there is marvelous, and he makes his own potato chips about as close to the same way as George Crum did as possible. The chef, Joe Shea, is an artisan, and his homemade chips are among the most popular in the whole city. In fact, the German movie crew that visited us went to the Stadium and filmed Joe making his original Saratoga Chips for his customers. And more recently, a Japanese film crew came and taped Joe making his chips also. I guess you could say that Joe Shea is an international superstar by now," she laughed.

Delicious Upstate New York Destinations

FAVORITE RESTAURANTS

I've always enjoyed reading restaurant reviews. I think the authors have a unique outlook on writing. Get in, get situated, survey the menu, critique the food, describe the ambiance, detail your impression of the place, and then (drum roll, please) give a thumbs-up or thumbs-down on the place. And then out. Talk about pressure! It really is a special talent.

Well, I'm now going to attempt my own star turn as a restaurant critic. Below are thirty eateries found all over Upstate New York. I've been to them all, and yes, I've enjoyed them all. Let me sharpen my No. 2 pencil, put on my green editor's visor, roll up my shirtsleeves, and give you my own thumbnail reviews of several places I think you might like to visit.

Albany: Jack's Oyster House. Gotta be the coziest place downtown. Jack's has been serving up oysters (and a lot more) since 1913. Waiters in white aprons tucked up under their armpits actually move the tables for you so you can squeeze into the booths. Power is in the air here, just down the hill from the Capitol. Many years ago, I saw Governor Rockefeller and his wife, Happy, come in for dinner while I was here.

Altamont: The Home Front Café. I have eaten at this cozy spot several times. The food is wonderful, with a just-like-Mom-used-to-make quality about it. The only problem for me is, I can never get out of this place. The whole restaurant is bathed in 1940s nostalgia. Served up as a tribute to World War II veterans, the café walls are chockablock with vintage sheet music, old photographs, uniforms, and military memorabilia. There is even a tank out front. Totally fascinating little spot, and a great place to bring your grand-kids. They'll enjoy listening in to the old timers share war stories in a place that looks like it has been lifted right out of a Norman Rockwell painting.

The author stands in front of a military vehicle outside of the World War II–themed Home Front Café in Altamont.

Barryville: Reber's Carriage House. My parents' favorite restaurant. They used to stay in Reber's Alpine cottages across the road for weekend getaways in the 1950s. They'd walk down the driveway to Reber's for a night of German food and live music. Because no alcohol was served in New York on Sundays back then, my folks and their friends would walk over the bridge and go to Rohmann's Bar in Shohola, Pennsylvania, which was built before the Civil War! Reber's (now The Carriage House) has changed a lot over the years, but the main room is the same as when old Herman Reber would welcome guests for dining a half century ago.

Big Indian: The Peekamoose Restaurant and Tap Room. Why would chefs who worked in such highfalutin places like New York City's La Bernadin and Gramercy Tavern move to the rural frontier of Upstate's border with Pennsylvania and open up a restaurant? Well, in this modern day version of *Green Acres* they did. It worked and we are all the better for it. Devin and Marybeth Mills have refashioned an old farmhouse in the Catskills into one of the most popular dining experiences you can find in the region. A lot of surprises once you enter Peekamoose, including their own cured pork tenderloins and a bar stocked with more than ninety international wines. It is all about farm-to-table at this elegantly rustic restaurant, which is one of the largest in the Catskills. Don't miss the nightly bonfire with an endless supply of marshmallows!

Binghamton: Little Venice. Binghamton has no shortage of wonderful Italian restaurants, but this has always been my favorite. The walls of the large dining room are filled with large, individually lit oil paintings giving this an aura of Old Italy. The homemade pasta is superb and the "meatlogs" are unmatched. Officious servers, some of whom have been here more than thirty years, keep things running smoothly at a frenetic pace during dinner hours. Hundreds of celebrities have stopped in here over the years, as witnessed by the many autographed photos on the walls.

Canastota: Graziano's World Famous Restaurant. Old World charm within sight of the National Boxing Hall of Fame. Tony Graziano had a storied career in boxing, but credit Mama Maria for these mouthwatering recipes. The eighty-foot-long bar is something to see. You can't miss this place. Exit the New York State Thruway at Canastota and you are looking right at it.

Cazenovia: The Brae Loch Inn. Stunning 1805 stone estate overlooking Cazenovia Lake. Turned into a full Scottish-themed hotel, inn, and restaurant in 1950. Oozes Gaelic charm. Display cases abound packed with Scottish memorabilia. Suits of armor stand at attention in the hallway, an ancient stone fireplace roars away in the lobby, and a Tartan plaid carpet covers the dining room floor. Restaurant seating is either at tables or comfortable booths. An open grill area allows you to observe your meal being prepared. Entrees include an excellent Scotch Smoked Salmon. And of course, haggis is a specialty. This lovely inn was the first place I ever spent the weekend away with my wife. Very romantic!

Cooperstown: The Otesaga Hotel. Since 1909, this imposing, columned, cupola-topped hotel has been the village's landmark structure. Located on the southern shore of Otsego Lake, it is just a short four-block stroll from the National Baseball Hall of Fame. The hotel offers several different dining options, all excellent, but no matter where you choose to eat here, one must end the day with a cocktail on the famous Otesaga

Veranda. This expansive porch, replete with placid lakeside vistas, welcoming Adirondack rocking chairs and an attentive waitstaff, is one of the signature experiences in the land of James Fenimore Cooper. Take a look at who is rocking away next to you. A movie star? A famous politician? A baseball Hall of Famer? You just never know . . .

Downsville: The Old Schoolhouse Inn and Restaurant. This building is great. Erected in 1903 as the community's first school, the Old Schoolhouse is a fully renovated inn and restaurant that totally evokes a bygone era. The main dining room and the upstairs banquet facilities are former classrooms. The ambiance is "immersive nostalgia" right down to the old tin ceilings and the polished wainscoting throughout. For one of the most unique dining treats in Upstate New York, order one of their famous Longhorn Burgers. Owners Tom and Julie Markert also own the nearby Triple M Ranch where they raise over two hundred head of registered Texas Longhorn cattle. You have heard of "farm-to-table"? Well, here it is "ranch-to-table."

Eagle Bay: Big Moose Inn. A classic Adirondack lodge tucked away in the pines. Overlooking Big Moose Lake. Menu is heavy on the beef side, perhaps as it should be here in the rugged mountains of Upstate New York. Steaks and chops are king. Try the Big Moose twenty-ounce slow-roasted Angus steak. Hearty is an understatement. Check out the tavern with its ten thousand business cards collected over the years and covering the entire ceiling. Oh, and hey. Look! Outside the dining room window. Down by the lake. It's a New York State historical marker! Be sure and stroll down and read it after your meal. It tells quite an amazing story about the "crime of the century," which took place here in 1906. Creepy.

Essex: The Old Dock House Restaurant. Housed in a two-hundred-year-old building on the western shore of Lake Champlain. Within walking distance of the Essex-Charlotte ferry to Vermont. A stunning locale for a steak dinner or just some cocktails and appetizers on the waterfront. Situated with the Green Mountains of Vermont in front of you, and the Adirondacks behind you. A great little spot.

Hancock: Hancock House Hotel. Comfortable restaurant in an impressive three-story hotel located near the Pennsylvania border. Meals in the Maple Room are delicious. Have a drink or a snack at the hotel's tavern. Called Honest Eddie's, the pub pays tribute to Hancock native Eddie Murphy, a star ballplayer with the Chicago White Sox. He played with Shoeless Joe Jackson in the infamous 1919 World Series Black Sox scandal and came out as the only untainted player. Hence the name. Honest Eddie was the very first batter to ever face a new pitcher named Babe Ruth. Some of Murphy's personal artifacts decorate the walls of the tavern.

Ithaca: The BoatYard Grill. They take great pride in preparing some of the best hand-cut steaks in Central New York, and they boast (deservedly so) of their impeccable selection of "fresh flown-in seafood," but Mother Nature gets the most credit here at the BoatYard. Comfortably situated on a spit of land that juts into the clear blue waters of Cayuga Lake, this is the best spot for dining and relaxing in this college city. Outdoor patios offer a truly stunning backdrop for an excellent meal in a city known for great food.

Kingston: Eng's Chinese Restaurant. Almost impossible to resist stopping at the old façade with the blazing art deco "Chop Suey" neon sign out front. Located on historic Broadway, Eng's is not only Kingston's oldest Chinese restaurant (1927) but one of the first Chinese restaurants in all of Upstate. Lots of original items on the menu (including chop suey, of course) and daily chef specials. A popular one is called Dragon and Phoenix, which is a combination of shrimp and chicken mixed with the chef's own white sauce. Also ask for Chef Hong Chan's prized Cantonese steak.

Little Falls: Beardslee Castle. One of Upstate's most unusual dining spots. Built in 1860 as a replica of an Irish castle, this place is darkly Gothic and stunningly beautiful at the same time. The landscaping in the spring and fall is gorgeous and makes for a beauteous backdrop for the many weddings held here. You can dine in the Dungeon Bar (if you dare). The History Channel came to Beardslee in 1999 to see if it is haunted. It is.

Mt. Upton: The Old Mill. In existence for seven decades, it is still one of those comfy places where they serve you a twirling relish tray and a crock of Wisconsin cheese with crackers as an appetizer. This has been a mill location for 250 years. Notice the fifteen-hundred-pound grinding stone that is on the riverside terrace behind the restaurant. I can't count the number of Mother's Day, Easter Sunday, or graduation day lunches I have had here.

New Paltz: Mohonk Mountain House. This is perhaps New York's most beautiful hotel. Really impossible to describe, the Mohonk is seemingly carved into the stony sides of the Shawangunk Mountains just outside of New Paltz. The hotel was founded by Albert Smiley in 1869 and is still owned by family members. The view from any of the 260 hotel rooms will take your breath away. No wonder five U.S. presidents have stayed here. I've dined at the Mohonk Mountain House several times, always at the Sunday brunch. It is legendary. Once you get over the sticker shock of the walk-in price (seventy-five dollars) you will find yourself under the towering, beamed roof of the main dining room confronting one of the most expansive arrays of foods, mostly local, ever assembled on one (or ten) serving tables. Carving stations abound, dessert displays are everywhere, giant bowls of fresh green salads anchor every table, fresh seafood and custom-made breakfast omelets vie for your attention. It is just like that. Everyone should do the Mohonk Sunday brunch at least once in their life.

Pine Plains: Stissing House Restaurant. Michel and Patricia Jean bring their years of culinary expertise to this venerable Hudson Valley restaurant. Serving some of the finest French cuisine found in the state. Lots of local beef, poultry and vegetables find their way to the tables of one of the oldest continuously operating restaurants in the nation. Stissing House sits regally on a corner and is topped with a distinctive wraparound second-floor balcony. The tavern is ancient and cozy.

Rhinebeck: The Beekman Arms. You should go here if for no other reason than this is the oldest continuously operating inn in America. Its colonial grandeur has graced a busy downtown corner of Rhinebeck since 1766. Nice place to begin a visit to this historic town. In the winter you will be enticed to stay and sit for a while by the nostalgic aroma emanating from several large crackling wood fireplaces in the dining room.

Rome: Vescio's Franklin Hotel. In a city overflowing with great restaurants, the Franklin serves the best bowl of spaghetti within the city limits. Hands down. Everything homemade. Not much to look at from the outside, but long lines will greet you on weekend nights and holidays. Superb.

Roscoe: The Roscoe Diner. If not the best diner in Upstate, certainly the most famous. I have eaten here probably twenty-five times in my life. I've never been disappointed. The sandwiches are Broadway big, the cakes and pies are positively Himalayan in size, and the free bowl of dill pickles there to greet you when you sit down lets you know you are in for a treat. Located halfway between Binghamton and New York City on NYS Route 17, this diner has fed thousands of migratory students who have pulled off at Roscoe, "Trout Town, USA."

Roxbury: The Public Lounge. Must be seen to be believed. Tony restaurant set in a TV Land setting of vivid colors and 1950s retro wonderfulness. As hip as you can get in the Catskill Mountains. The menu is high end. Bok choy or Arctic char with chervil sauce, anyone? National magazines have found this eatery and raved about it. Attached is the famous Roxbury Motel with its imaginatively themed guest rooms. Yes, you can stay in a Partridge Family Room or even a Star Trek Room. And all of this in a rural town, population twenty-five hundred, with Victorian homes and tall white church steeples. Like I said . . . must be seen to be believed.

Saranac Lake: Eat 'n Meet Grill and Larder. This *Mayberry R.F.D.*–named restaurant is the perfect match for the small town atmosphere of this lakeside community. This favorite is nestled in a much-added-to, turn-of-the-century-style general store. You can eat inside or out on the deck. The chef, John Vargo, is one of the Adirondacks' best. Ever hear of lobster mushrooms? They've got them, and people love them! Make a reservation, this place gets crowded. Located just a couple blocks from the stores and the lake.

Saratoga Springs: Hattie's Restaurant. An Upstate landmark if ever there was one. Hattie's has been serving up Southern fried soul food and Louisiana cuisine since 1938. Lots of New Orleans flavors here. Beignets, crab cakes, biscuits and gravy, grits, and Hattie's famous fried chicken (same recipe since the day the place opened) are the stars of the menu. Hattie Moseley-Austen passed away in 1998 at nearly one hundred years of age, but her sense of taste, style, and congeniality live on in the present owners. Of particular interest is Hattie's neighbor in the same building. Caffè Lena is the oldest operating coffee house in the United States and was the first place Bob Dylan ever performed outside of New York City.

Seneca Falls: The Gould Hotel. On the same location for nearly a century, this hotel was named after the Gould Pump Manufacturing Company, which was founded and is still located in town. Elegant restaurant serving everything from Yankee pot roast to sole to filet mignon. A perfect launching place for a walking tour of this historic village. The National Women's Hall of Fame is just down the street. Walk down Main Street at night. Look familiar? It is said that movie director Frank Capra based his classic Christmas film *It's A Wonderful Life* on this village, which he had visited.

Sharon Springs: The American Hotel: Sharon Springs was once a mecca for downstate tourists who came here for the mineral water cures. This little village has slowly emerged as a destination vacation for many folks looking for quiet country relaxation with a little touch of Hollywood. The American Hotel was built in 1837 but was abandoned and neglected for decades until Garth Roberts and Doug Plummer bought it in 1996 for less than twenty thousand dollars. A small fortune later, this place has been recognized and honored as a sterling example of high preservation. The restaurant serves everything from fresh Maine lobster to a three-cheese stuffed crepe. The *New York Times* has reviewed the hotel's restaurant, and TV's favorite food star Rachel Ray featured it on her show and said the charbroiled lamb chops in garlic sauce were "the tops." Josh and Brent, television's *Fabulous Beekman Boys* and the winners of the reality show *The Amazing Race*, own a mercantile right across the street.

Skaneateles: The Sherwood Inn. Total class. Extensive menu and comfortable pub. Everything is top notch. This hulking green inn and restaurant anchors the western edge of Skaneateles's historic and quaint lakeside downtown. Go on a festival day (of which there are many) to really experience the wonder of this Finger Lakes gem.

Syracuse: Mother's Cupboard. Hailed by locals as the best breakfast in the city. Long the workingman's friend, this restaurant recently went viral with the students of SU and other local colleges. The main drawing card is the famous Mother's Cupboard Frittata Challenge. Six pounds of food shoved on to a large plate. With bacon, fried onions, eggs, rolls, pepperoni, sausage, broccoli, red peppers, and hash browns staring back at you, this challenge is not for the faint of heart. Adam Richman, the host of TV's *Man v. Food*, took the challenge and beat it (barely).

Troy: Muza. Polish and Hungarian made-from-scratch food. Great little spot near Rensselaer Polytechnic Institute. Menu is heavy with (no pun intended) satisfying meals evocative of a time when plates arrived at your table filled to the edges, and the only thing "lite" on the menu was the price. A cup of homemade Hungarian goulash with red peppers and onions (under five dollars), six generous Polish potato, cheese and onion pierogies (eleven dollars). All good deals. But, heck. Why not just go for the gusto and order the Polish Feast? Pierogies, stuffed cabbages, kielbasas, mashed potatoes, and more. And just sixteen dollars. Wash it all down with an ice cold Zywiec (Polish beer) in the beer garden. Nice touch.

Utica: Delmonico's Italian Steak House. There are several Delmonico's restaurants scattered across Upstate. I've only dined at the Utica venue and I really enjoyed it. The food is excellent and the portions are ample. And the prices aren't too bad either. However, it is the decorated restaurant walls that keep me coming back for another look over. Hundreds of life-sized caricatures grace every inch of wall space in the public area, offering a delightful *Where's Waldo?* kind of guessing game while you are waiting for your dinner. Italian American actors (Marlon Brando), singers (Dean Martin), sports legends (Mario Andretti), and politicians (Governor Cuomo) all stare back at you in a whimsical homage to the tradition of caricature-lined walls made famous on Broadway at Sardis. Nothing like working your way through their signature twenty-four-ounce Angus steak while being ogled by a six-foot-tall image of Sophia Loren!

FUN FOOD FESTIVALS

*U*pstate New York is the land of festivals. Every little town has one as does every major city. For many years I have hosted a website that looks at the festivals in the Empire State (www.newyorkstatefestivals.com). This website has allowed me to travel all over the state experiencing the best of our state festivals. Not surprisingly, many of the best are our food festivals.

With New York's burgeoning wine and microbrew industries, many festivals are now centered around these two beverages. I have tried to keep my list focused more on the foods of Upstate New York. Also, our region is a veritable melting pot of ethnic diversity. Because of this you are sure to find excellent food opportunities at the many Polish, Italian, German, and other ethnic gatherings throughout the year.

Below I have listed information about a select group of the very best festivals held in all four seasons throughout our region. I have been to almost all of them. I invite you to visit my festival website and let me know if I have missed one in your town!

(*Author's Note*: Festivals are famous for changing their dates. Sometimes venues move, crowds get bigger, or better availabilities open up. Be sure to check out the websites of these and all festivals before going).

Apple Festival: There are several apple festivals around the state (in Warwick, Hilton, Altamont, Schodack, and Ithaca, for example), but the granddaddy of them all is the Lafayette Apple Festival (Onondaga County). The region just south of Syracuse is one of the primary apple orchard areas in the state. This event has grown so large that many out-of-state motor coach companies now schedule runs from Pennsylvania, Massachusetts, and Vermont. More than one hundred thousand attend in late summer

Close to one hundred thousand visitors attend this festival every year. Motor coaches bring tourists from all over the Northeast to sample Central New York's apples.

or early fall, making this one of the biggest festivals, food or otherwise, in New York State.

AppleUmpkin Festival: Although the focus here is on regional arts and crafts, AppleUmpkin also has a wide array of apple and pumpkin food samplings to enjoy. The town of Wyoming (in the county of the same name) is located in the fertile Dale Valley area, known for its rich harvest of apples and pumpkins, among other items. The festival, started in 1968, now draws more than ten thousand visitors. A highlight is the annual bake-off. Contestants have three categories: Apple, pumpkin, or (of course) AppleUmpkin! Check out the chapter about apple sausage for more on the festival. The festival is held at the end of September.

Bacon Fest: This is one of Upstate's fastest growing festivals. After its first year it had to move from its original venue, a park in Hudson, New York, upriver to Troy (Rensselaer County), where it has been incorporated into the popular Troy Pig Out. Between fifteen and twenty thousand bacon lovers descend on Troy's beautiful Riverfront Park for a day of live music, barbecue cook-off contests, and weird food (bacon flavored ice cream?). The festival is held in July.

Bagel Festival: Monticello (Orange County) was named the Bagel Capital by a proclamation of the New York State Legislature. The festival here features live music, a Bagel Star Parade, a bagel triathlon (where the doughy rolls are stacked, tossed, and thrown), and a bagel art contest. A highlight is trying to set the world record for the largest bagel chain down Main Street (the goal is five thousand bagels strung on a rope). The bagel-making machine was invented nearby in 1966, hence the "capital" assignment. Get your schmear on at this festival, which attracts ten thousand visitors. It is held in August.

Cheese Festival: There are several cheese festivals in the state, but this one in Monroe (Orange County) is unique in that it takes place in the birthplace of Velveeta Cheese! The original Velveeta building still stands in downtown Monroe at 30 Millpond Parkway. The festival features live bands, fun for kids, food and vendor tents, and a wine and cheese party. As they say in Monroe, "Have a cheesetastic day!" About four thousand attend this festival, which is held in September.

Chicken Wing Festival: The single biggest food festival in Upstate New York. Its roots stem from an old Bill Murray movie, *Osmosis Jones*, which tells the story of a person on the hunt for the National Chicken Wing Festival. Only problem was . . . there was no such festival. Now there is, and it takes over the entire city of Buffalo (Erie County) when it is held. Nearly one hundred thousand people attend the weekend event. So far the festival, which is held in the birth city of the chicken wing, has cooked up more than two million chicken wings, has donated more than $250 thousand to Buffalo charities, and has grown so large that it now takes over Coca Cola Field, home to the minor league baseball team the Buffalo Bisons. The festival is held Labor Day weekend.

Chili Festival: Something about the month of February in Upstate New York brings out the chili fest in all of us. Ithaca (Tompkins County) has the biggest of them all. The city has unique festival grounds for it, too: the Commons is a pedestrian plaza in the heart of downtown that hosts several festivals a year, and this one brings more than ten thousand visitors. The event is ostensibly a chili cook-off, and for a small price attendees wander the area sampling everything from rattlesnake chili to venison chili. With a couple of major colleges in the city (Cornell and Ithaca College), this is a popular food festival with young people. It is held every February.

Chocolate Train Wreck Festival: Though it is now known officially as the Great Chocolate Festival, locals still refer to this event as the "train wreck festival." This fun community gathering commemorates an actual event. On September 27, 1955, an Ontario and Western railroad train was speeding through town when it jumped the tracks and crashed. Nobody was hurt. It did, however, spill its contents all over the area. The contents? Hundreds of units of Nestle Quik drink mix, dozens of boxes of chocolate chips, thousands of Nestle Crunch candy bars, and more. Local children raced to the scene and scrambled over the chocolate heaps to make off with their bounty. The festival is held in the beautiful village green in the center of Hamilton (Madison County), just a block away from Colgate University. Several eyewitnesses to the train wreck (now all adults) are usually on hand to share their personal stories of the Chocolate Train Wreck of 1955. The festival is held in September.

Chowderfest: This has become one of the largest food festivals in the state. Thousands come to historic Saratoga each year to sample (for one dollar a cup) dozens of chowder offerings. Chowder cooking stations line the streets, sidewalks, alleys, storefronts, and parking lots during this one-day event. Choices run from corn chowder to clam chowder to elk chowder and everything in between. This festival is held in February.

Corn Festival: The Eden Corn Festival is another one of Upstate's long traditions. It began in 1963. The festival features a large parade with over seventy-five marching units, craft shows, live entertainment, an auto show, a Queen Corn contest and, of course, a corn husking contest. Thousands of ears of corn are cooked up and served at the festival every year. Eden (Erie County) is in the middle of a huge corn growing area of Western New York. The festival is held the first weekend in August.

Cream Cheese Festival: This festival celebrates Lowville's distinction of being the home to the world's largest cream cheese manufacturing plant at Kraft Foods. More than fifteen thousand people make their way to this rural North Country village (Lewis County) every year to enjoy the festival and to participate in the making of the world's largest cheese-cake. The *Guinness Book of World Records* has certified the festival's most recent cheesecake as the titleholder, coming in at 6,900 pounds and making more than 24,500 slices available to sell to the festival crowd and to donate to the local food pantry. The festival is held in September.

Cupcake Festival: Perfect for those with a sweet tooth. Little Gardiner (Ulster County) showcases more than thirty thousand cupcakes for your pleasure, with something for every taste. There are cupcake decorating contests, carnivals, live music, a Cupcake 5K Run, and a tasting contest. The festival is held at the beautiful 450-acre, century-old Wrights Farm in town. This is another one of the newer, faster-growing festivals in Upstate.

Empire State Plaza Food Festival: Granted, the focus here is live music with national names entertaining the crowd, but the food selections are pretty awesome, too. What really sets this Albany (Albany County) food festival apart from others is the magnificent setting it is in. More than fifty specialty vendors (food and nonfood) set up around the reflecting pool at the stunning Empire State Plaza. The old capitol building is at one end, and the soaring Corning Tower (the tallest building in the state outside of New York City) is at the other. A nice event in a very nice setting. This festival is held in August.

Food Truck Festival: Food trucks are a fairly new phenomenon in Upstate New York. This festival features more than two dozen food trucks corralled along the Hudson River in Troy (Rensselaer County). Vendors serve a wide variety of foods right from their truck windows, including barbecue, desserts, ethnic cuisine, and more. Some favorites include the Wandering Dago (Italian food), Slidin' Dirty (gourmet slider sandwiches), and Pies on Wheels (a have-to-see-it-to-believe-it, self-contained, custom pizza kitchen on wheels). The festival is held in May.

Garlic Festival: The Hudson Valley Garlic Festival in Saugerties (Ulster County) is one of many garlic celebrations around Upstate. Others are held in Milford, Cuba, Penn Yan, and Little Falls, where they have the clever saying "Eat, Stink and Be Merry." The Saugerties festival is the biggest and features dozens of garlic vendors and a full lineup of live entertainment. In the Garlic Marketplace you can buy items such as garlic clove candles, garlic ice cream, garlic pickles, and garlic jellies.

The festival began as a single day event in 1989, but by 1995 it was drawing more than fifty thousand visitors and producing an eleven-mile-long backup on the New York State Thruway. It was then changed to a two-day event. It is held in September.

Grape Festival: This Ontario County festival honors the rich grape-growing harvest of the Finger Lakes region. Since it began in 1961, the festival has been held every September to celebrate the glorious grape, which is abundant in the Naples area. Naples is so proud of its high quality grapes that even the fire hydrants in the village are painted purple in a tribute to this signature crop! The World's Greatest Grape Pie Contest is always a highlight. Monica's Pie Shop (see chapter 8) is always a contender.

Italian Cheese Festival: Officially a street festival (in fact, the second largest Italian street festival in the United States) this Buffalo food festival is sponsored by Galbani Cheese (it was originally sponsored and known as the Sorrento Cheese Festival). Many choices of Italian food, all thick with great Italian cheeses, are available to the thousands who attend this festival. It is held in North Buffalo's Little Italy (Erie County). Among the many highlights of the event are the daily grape-stomping exhibit and the popular cooking stages, which feature local and national Italian chefs. The festival is held in July.

Maple Festival: The Central New York Maple Festival is held in Marathon (Cortland County). A total celebration of New York's famed maple production, this festival has been going on for more than four decades. It includes a pancake eating contest, a Maple Queen pageant, an arts and crafts show, live music, and a pancake-eating contest. Thousands attend. It is held in mid-April.

Onion Festival: A little-known fact is that Elba (Genesee County) calls itself the Onion Capital of the World. Mucklands, swampy areas drained of water, are ripe for the growing of onions, and Elba sits in one of the largest mucklands in the East. This is one of New York's oldest festivals, beginning in 1937. The festival has all of the usual events, from parades to music to food (and lots of onions!), but it is also notable for having given away a car every year in a raffle. That's right, more than seventy-five cars have been given away since the festival began! This festival is held in early August.

Peach Festival: This event has been held in Lewiston (Niagara County) for more than fifty years. More than fifty thousand people attend the festival, which features an eye-popping display of the area's sumptuous peach harvest. A parade, carnival, and live entertainment stage keep the activities fun for all. There is a Peach Queen pageant as well as a Peach Fuzz contest. Of course, the peach cook-off is highly anticipated. Samples of peach cobbler and peach shortcake are on every corner. One of the newest additions is a Peach 5K Run. It is held every September.

Pickle Festival: The International Pickle Festival is held in Rosendale (Ulster County). More than eight thousand people pucker up and attend this festival, which is now more than fifty years old. You can buy almost anything pickled here: pickled pineapple, fried pickles, pickle ice cream and (cue the pucker), a whole dill pickle covered with chocolate, and M&M candies! This festival takes place in November.

Pie Festival: The Jennie Bell Pie Festival in Accord (Ulster County) is named after one of the areas earliest settlers. Jennie Bell was famous for contributing her homemade pies to every imaginable community effort, and this pie festival is her legacy. More than three thousand visitors attend the festival, which began in 2004. The Best Pie competition is fiercely contested by the good bakers in the Hudson Valley. Fireworks cap this fun event. It is held in September.

Potato Festival: There are several festivals in Upstate honoring the lowly spud, including those in Wayland and Richford. But I would have to go with this one in Savannah (Wayne County), if for no other reason than it features mashed potato wrestling! There is also a children's beauty pageant (Miss Tater Tot), potato bowling, potato peeling contests, and a potato gun shooting competition. Kids like to scour the festival area searching for the "golden potato" and all the prizes it brings with it. The festival is held in September (there's no website, so check Facebook for an accurate date).

Ramp Festival: A ramp is one of the earliest of the annual leeks. This springtime member of the onion family is abundant in the Hudson Valley and is a favorite of chefs around the world. RampFest is held in Hudson, NY (Columbia County), in a historic old building known as the Hudson Basilica. This former manufacturing facility hosts dozens of food vendors, live entertainment, and arts and crafts during the festival. The air is filled with the aromatic zing of ramps being cooked, fried, and sautéed as regional chefs (and some from as far away as New York City) prepare dishes for the festival goers to enjoy. RampFest began in 2000 and continues to grow each year. It is held near the end of April or beginning of May every year.

Rhubarb Festival: This festival is held at the Montezuma Winery, one of the Finger Lakes' most popular. Hundreds come to Seneca Falls (Seneca County) to attend this one-of-a-kind festival and enjoy rhubarb candies, rhubarb chili, and (of course) homemade rhubarb pie. The winery has tastings and sales throughout the event. This festival is held in the summer.

Riggiefest: The chicken riggie, a popular dish found in the Utica-Rome area, is featured in chapter 17. Teddy's Restaurant won Riggiefest's Best of Show award three times and retired from competition. The festival is now held at the Utica Memorial Auditorium (Oneida County). Thousands attend every year, all to benefit the Utica area YWCA. It was first held in 2005. Date fluctuates so check the website for details.

Sauerkraut Festival: Phelps (Ontario County) was once known as the Sauerkraut Capital of the World. The festival began in 1966 and features such unusual events as cabbage bowling, sauerkraut eating contests and the crowning of the Kraut King and Queen. If you attend, you have to try a slice of their famous sauerkraut cake! The festival is held the first weekend in August.

Spiedie Fest: The focus here is the spiedie sandwich, which is native to Binghamton (see chapter 19). The festival is held in Otsiningo Park (Broome County) and features a balloon launch, national name entertainment, and nearly two hundred food vendors. The festival began in 1983 and four thousand people attended. Now nearly one hundred thousand attend annually. It is held the first full weekend in August.

Strawberry Festival: Hundreds of thousands of visitors have poured into Owego (Tioga County) to enjoy this summertime festival since it began in 1980. More than two hundred vendors line the streets of downtown Owego selling their wares, which are heavy on the food side. Of course, the official dish of this festival is strawberry shortcake, and thousands of these desserts are sold on festival day. It is held in June.

Tomato Festival: This is one of the few New York festivals held at a state park. Evangola State Park in Irving (Erie County) is home to one of the only statewide festivals honoring the tomato. Events include the biggest tomato competition, tomato-eating contests, best homemade tomato sauce, and even a best tomato costume contest. A new event is the 5K Tomato Trot. This event is held in August.

Utica Greens Festival: This festival is held in conjunction with the annual Utica Music and Arts Festival. Utica greens, one of this city's most popular creations, are a spicy, Southern Italian side dish made of escarole, prosciutto, cheese, roasted potatoes, and red peppers (with a thousand different variations). The delicacy is sold in almost every restaurant in Utica (Oneida County). This festival is very heavily into live music (with as many as three performing stages), but if you have never tried Utica's signature dish this would be a great place to sample some of the best the city has to offer. The festival is held in September.

INDEX